AL CAPONE
stories my grandmother told me

AL CAPONE
stories my grandmother told me

—— *for the first time* ——
the true stories of Al Capone's private life
written by his granddaughter

DIANE PATRICIA CAPONE

Book design by Jessika Hazelton • The Troy Book Makers
Troy, New York • thetroybookmakers.com
Originally printed by The Troy Book Makers in the United States of America

To order additional copies of this title,
contact your favorite local bookstore
or visit www.shoptbmbooks.com

ISBN: 978-1-61468-539-5

This book is dedicated to my sister,
Veronica Capone Peterson,

To my grandparents,
Mary Josephine "Mae" Coughlin
and Alphonse Gabriel Capone,

And to my parents,
Diana Ruth Casey and
Albert Francis "Sonny" Capone

"Always Alive in My Heart"

CONTENTS

INTRODUCTION

MY GRANDFATHER WAS AL CAPONE. He married my grandmother, Mary Josephine Coughlin (Mae), three weeks after the birth of their only child, my father, Albert Francis Capone. Albert (known as Sonny all his life) was the father of four daughters: Veronica Francis, Diane Patricia (I was always called Pat within the family), Barbara Mae and Theresa Marie. We lost our beloved Veronica (Ronnie) eleven years ago. I am the eldest living granddaughter. There are some nieces and nephews (my second cousins) still alive, but my sisters and I are Al Capone's closest living relatives and along with our children and their children, his only direct descendants.

We were raised in Miami, Florida, not far from my grandparents' house on Palm Island. For the first several years of our lives, my sister Ronnie and I spent as much time at the Island home of our grandparents as we did at our own. Al and Mae, always called Papa and Mama Mae by my sisters and me, were the epitome of adoring grandparents. We lived a very private life, and despite attempts by the media, the FBI and the insatiably curious to find out anything about our grandfather and his family, we were sheltered from public attention. We attended St. Mary's Catholic School and later Notre Dame Academy for girls, both located in Miami. We left Florida in the early 1960's after our parents separated, and we moved with our mother, Diana Ruth Casey, always called Casey, to California. My grandfather had been dead for eleven years by the time we left. Had he still lived, I doubt that the separation would have occurred and we would probably still be living in Florida. I say this because my grandfather adored my mother. Despite his own marital mistakes, he would have insisted that his son, Sonny, not make any of those same mistakes. The family must always come first.

To my knowledge, there are no other descendants of my grandfather or his siblings alive today who were born with the Capone name on their birth certificates other than my sisters and me. As the years have gone by, all my sisters and I have married and so the "Capone" name has been put to rest. We are certainly aware of the unauthorized use of my grandfather's name by vendors all over the world, and the desire by some people to try to make money through claims of a connection to him. We have been offended by some and often amused by others, but we always kept still. All our family stories were kept private until now.

So why break the silence at all? There are three answers. First, I am writing this memoir for me and my loved ones as an attempt to set straight the personal story of my grandparents and my family, and to honor my late sister, Veronica Capone Peterson. Of all his descendants, Ronnie inherited the best of my grandfather's personality. She was every bit as brilliant, as charismatic, as generous, as fiercely loyal and devoted to family as Papa was. She even had his musical ability. She embodied all the qualities of his nature except violence.

My grandfather's stature as a figure in American history has grown so much since his death that there doesn't seem to be any place on earth where Al Capone's name is not recognized. Like many other public figures, famous or infamous, the more mystery there is surrounding a person's life the more curious people become. Unfortunately, when some people don't know the truth, they tend to make it up.

This story is not made up. It is the truth as I know it, based on my own memories, on the stories my grandmother told me, the diaries my mother kept, and the memories of my father and of the other family members who were alive during the lives of my grandfather and grandmother. Until recently, no one ever knew about Al Capone's final days or what happened to his family. Answers to those questions and others will be found in this book.

The second answer to "why break the silence" is that after the deaths of my grandparents, my parents, and more recently my sister Ronnie, I realize how fragile our lives are. If I am ever going to write our story, I cannot wait, and as I am the only one still alive who can do it, I have to speak for all of us, to tell all our stories.

My grandfather did some really bad things during his early years and paid a high price for those things. This is not an attempt to obscure the facts or to gloss over the horrible times. Nor is it my intention to rationalize his behavior. There are some well written books that deal with his public life during the era of Prohibition far more comprehensively than I ever could. This memoir focuses on what happened in Al's private life that was not covered in the newspapers. It discusses his life-long love affair with Mae, and describes who he became after his public life ended. It also answers some of the most often asked questions about him and his family. What was Al Capone really like? How did he die? What happened to all his money? What was his mysterious wife Mae like? What happened to his family? There are some secrets that should not be relegated to the grave.

As his closest living relative and the only person still alive who was in the room with him in Al Capone's final hours, I will share my remembrances. As I have already mentioned, my sister Ronnie and I spent a good bit of our childhood living at his home on Palm Island, and after we grew up, we became the primary confidantes of his wife, Mae Capone. At last, some of the stories my grandmother told me will be shared.

In researching this memoir I was lucky to discover journals written by my mother, which cover some of the days after Al Capone returned to Florida. Her wonderful stories fill in some of the gaps between her first meeting with my grandfather in 1940 and years later, when my own memories occur. My mother's journals also recount her early years in Miami Beach and tell about falling in love with my father, Sonny, which I believe greatly enrich the memoir.

Three of my favorite relatives also provided eye witness accounts of those days in Florida before Ronnie and I were born. Our dear Aunt Winnie Coughlin (Al's sister-in-law) who is now deceased, loved to tell stories of Miami Beach in the early forties and about my grandparents and the festivities at their home on Palm Island. My Uncle James F. Casey (my mother's only brother), who until his death a few months ago, was very encouraging and always supportive of this story finally being told. My Uncle Jim was eleven when he met my grandfather and until my grandfather died in 1947, Jim was a constant visitor at his island home. And finally, my cousin Clairmae (Mae Capone's niece) who is very much alive, shared colorful tales of many happy times with my grandparents on the Island. Clairmae grew up in Chicago and often spent whole summers at the Capone home on Palm Island when she was a young teenager. She told me, "My favorite memories of Uncle Al were how he doted on his granddaughters and what a happy house it was, always filled with the sounds of laughter and music." He would often say, "Aren't they the most beautiful girls in the world?" "The truth is he made all of us feel beautiful," Clairmae would say.

Al Capone has been called a Cultural Icon; Public Enemy No. 1; the John D. Rockefeller of the underworld; Robin Hood; and "Papa" among other things. In the 1930's he made the cover of Time Magazine. He also was listed in a 2014 issue of the Smithsonian magazine as one of the hundred most influential Americans in the history of the country. Is Al Capone more of an enigma than most powerful and well-known historical figures? Probably not. Most intelligent people have multifaceted personalities, and sometimes those facets are highly contradictory. Is he somehow more contradictory, more brilliant, more ruthless, or more colorful? Well, maybe. You decide.

How could this purported "king of the underworld" and an alleged killer be capable of such extraordinary kindness and generosity, such devotion to family and such loyalty to friends? How did a boy of working class Italian immigrants with nothing more than a sixth-grade education manage to build and lead a multimillion dollar illegal empire? My father often told us that, "it was rumored at one time that his father had more people on his payroll than the standing army of the United States."

Al Capone has been analyzed by some of the best minds in psychology and written about by hundreds of authors. In the seventy years since his death, interest in him has grown exponentially. Deirdre Bair, in her recent biography of my grandfather, cites many of the various forms in which public interest in him is illustrated. They run the gamut from television shows such as "Boardwalk Empire": to college courses entitled "Al Capone", which always fill up; to "Al Capone Festivals"; to postage stamps with his or Mae's visage on them in Tajikistan, amongst many other examples. Harvard University offered a graduate business course in which a case study explicitly examines the structure of the Capone organizational chart making useful extrapolations for legitimate corporate enterprises. Whether it is naming one's Pitbull "Al Capone" or wearing t-shirts with his image on them, he is better known today than he was during his lifetime. The interesting phenomenon is that he is more often seen in today's celebrity-crazed world as a hero, not as an antihero. It is obvious that interest in him and curiosity about his life is not diminishing. I hope this personal glimpse of him from his family's perspective will offer some new insights into Al Capone, the man I called "Papa."

While references will be made in this memoir to my dearest "little sisters": Barbara (Babs) and Theresa (Terri), I have deliberately not included their stories or perspectives in this book. They are both alive and capable of telling their own stories if they choose to. They have the right to their privacy and I would never presume to infringe on that. They also were not present when most of these stories were told to me. Even though Ronnie and I were not that much older chronologically, we always called ourselves "the big kids", and we always believed that we lived in a slightly different generation from my younger sisters, whom we called "the little kids".

These are stories my grandmother told me. They are stories my father told me. They are the stories and memories that my sister, Ronnie and I shared over the final months of her life. While no definitive portrait of another human being is possible, I will try to paint the truest picture I can of Al Capone, my beloved "Papa". As I already indicated, the focus will be on his personal life and not on what was covered in the newspapers. He would have had to live ten lives to do half of what has been recounted in the press.

I will share also the story of Mae Capone, his extraordinary wife and my grandmother. I will include stories of my parents, Casey and Sonny, and of Ronnie and me. Someone needs finally to tell the true story, that heartbreaking, wild, glorious story of Al, Mae, Casey, Sonny and my sister Ronnie.

Lastly, this is written in tribute to all the remarkable women in the Capone family: my grandmother, my mother and particularly my sister, Veronica Capone Peterson, arguably the best of the Capones.

chapter one
THE NIGHT PAPA DIED

AL CAPONE, MY BELOVED "PAPA", was an unforgettable man. I have many happy memories of him from my childhood, but the memory of the event that occurred on January 25, 1947, which changed all our lives, is not a happy one. This is exactly how I remember that winter night. My older sister Ronnie and I were wakened in what felt like the middle of the night and quickly dressed by our mother. We were carried hurriedly out to the two-door Chevy coupe parked in our driveway while our parents quietly reassured us that everything was all right. We were told we were going to the Island to see Papa. Such a night-time visit had never occurred before, but any time we got to go to visit our Papa was magical and we were two sleepy little girls who didn't question it.

The drive to Palm Island was a short one and there was little traffic at this hour. Our grandparents lived on an island in Miami Beach not far from where we lived. Papa always called our small white bungalow in Miami Shores "the little white house" and came to visit us regularly. As we drove, I looked back and forth at my parents and wondered about this strange visit. I did not ever remember seeing Daddy's usual smiling face so still. We arrived at what we called "Papa's bridge" within minutes and as we crossed that bridge we could see in the distance our grandparents' big house all aglow. Daddy drove toward the house and turned into the driveway. Instantly the big iron gates were opened. Our dear friend Daniel Brown, who was the caretaker, had been watching for our car, and as the gates opened he stepped aside so that we could enter. I noticed that the circular drive way was filled with cars and Brown wasn't smiling at us like he usually did. He looked away quickly as if seeing us was painful. Brown had been part of the family since my grandfather had bought the house in 1928. He had been a young man then, whose primary job was to supervise the gardeners and maintenance people. He had been a faithful and diligent employee all the years my father was growing up, and now was thought of not as staff, but as a member of the family. I had never seen his gentle brown face without a big welcoming smile before.

As soon as the car stopped, Daddy jumped out of it and raced through the front door of the house. This was very strange. We almost never went in through the front door. We always entered through the doors of the long screen porches that flanked the house. Also Daddy didn't help us out of the car but left Brown and our mother to see to us. All was eerily quiet. We could hear people moving around speaking in hushed voices, but there was no music, no laughter, and no big hugs from our grandparents to greet us. In the few minutes it took us to get out of the car and come into our grandparents' house, Daddy had disappeared. Our mother held our hands and guided us quickly to the stairway. She said softly, "Come my darlings, Papa is waiting for you." I remember so vividly the sadness on her face. My mother was wearing a dress, as were Ronnie and I. I was holding on to Mommy's left hand and Ronnie held her right as we began the climb. We had never climbed those stairs before. Always before, one of our parents or grandparents carried us. I remember clinging to Mommy's hand and how difficult it was for me to lift my short little-girl legs to climb each of those tall stairs. Mommy kept encouraging us repeating, "Come on girls, Papa is waiting for you". This was a strange night to be sure.

When we reached the top of the stairs we turned to the left and entered my grandparents' suite. We walked down the long mirrored bedroom hallway where Mama Mae's beautiful satin-covered dressing table stood against the wall. Everything in Mama Mae and Papa's room was in shades of ivory and peach. The furniture was white Louis XIV with gold-leaf trim, and there were crystal lighting sconces between the windows and along the hall and chandeliers that lighted our way. In the bedroom itself the lights were dimmer.

There were several people in the large bedroom, but it was very quiet. People only whispered to each other. Papa's mother, Grandma Capone, was there as was Aunt Maffie, Papa's sister, and some of Papa's brothers. Mama Mae had her silver rosary beads in her hand and was quietly crying on her sister, Muriel's, shoulder. She did not get up when we entered, and seemed unaware that we were even there. Daddy was leaning over Papa, who was lying on my grandparents' big bed and quietly whispering to him. Daddy turned when he saw us and his eyes were glittering with tears. Papa looked very pale and still, not at all the way he usually looked when he played with us. We had just been here a few days before to celebrate my birthday which fell on January 14th and his, which was a few days later on the 17th. He had been laughing and happy and had held me on his lap. He didn't look at all like he did now. Papa slowly turned his head toward us and as soon as he saw Ronnie and me, he smiled and reached for us. Daddy lifted Ronnie up onto the bed first, and then me, to kiss him. He smiled at me and I kissed him on both cheeks the way he always kissed me. Papa said, "I love you, baby girl," and I responded as I always did, "I love you more". That was the last time I ever saw his face. We were taken from the bedroom after a few minutes and he died within a matter of hours.

I am sure that we were told later that he had died and gone to heaven, and there must have been many tears shed, but I remember only what I have stated. That night, climbing those stairs, walking into his bedroom, and his words, "I love you, baby girl" are indelibly imprinted in my mind and have been all my life.

In the following days, my mother and father flew to Chicago with the other relatives for Papa's funeral. Ronnie and I stayed at home in Miami Shores with our nanny and our little sister, Babs. What I also do remember is that in the coming months, everything seemed to have changed at the Island. All the furniture in the grand living room was covered with sheets. The door to the dining room was closed, and our family never used that beautiful room again. There never was another giant Christmas tree twinkling in the living room as there had been just a few weeks before.

Eventually, there were good times and laughter at Mama Mae's home, but nothing was ever again as it had been. Guests were limited to family and the very closest friends. Mama Mae's hair changed from platinum blond to white, and even though she was only in her late forties, she never glowed with youthful vibrancy again. Papa was the soul of that house. His bigger than life persona filled every inch of it as well as the grounds. When he was gone, life seemed to also leave the house.

Al and Mae Capone at Palm Island with three granddaughters, Christmas 1946

Al Capone had been a big man in every sense of the word: his appetite for life, his big heart, his capacity for joy and certainly his stature. Al was close to six feet tall by his early teens, had broad shoulders and huge hands. By his late twenties he weighed well over 200 pounds and with some slight fluctuation, stayed that size throughout his life. At a time when the average male in the United States was five feet eight inches tall and weighed 144 pounds, Al was almost always the biggest man in the room. Despite his size, he was also agile and graceful. Except for the brief few months in 1940 when he first returned to his home on Palm Island after his incarceration and hospitalization, he never appeared to be physically diminished. He was a man who loved life and reveled in his role of family man, particularly being a grandfather.

Furthermore, when his doctors told my grandmother and his family shortly after his return to Florida that Al was not as robust as he appeared, she simply refused to believe it. His primary physician, Dr. Kenneth Phillips, said there was no way Al would ever be physically or mentally as he had once been, but he was stable and with good care could possibly live many years. That was all Mae needed to hear. She would never allow herself to believe the doctors' initial prognosis for Al. Dr. Phillips warned her that she also needed to take care of herself, but she would not listen to his words of caution either. Since the day in November 1939 when they had finally been reunited after over eight years apart, Mae had devoted every waking moment to making sure that Al had everything he wanted and the best care possible. She convinced herself that she could extend his life by sheer determination, and even if it shortened her own life, Al was all that mattered to her. My grandmother put on her rose colored glasses and proclaimed to all that, "Al would be fine."

We children knew nothing of his health issues and to us he was just our wonderful always loving "Papa", a giant of a man with a giant heart.

I never remember seeing him without a smile on his face. That vivid memory of his smiling face was to be another of the most indelible memories of my life.

Those happy images of Papa and our times together in his wonderful island home are still with me now all these years later. The fragrance of a gardenia instantly transports me to my grandparents' home where tubs of that pungent lovely white flower lined the driveway. My grandmother always said Papa was happiest when he was holding one of his granddaughters or walking with us throughout his gardens. He told us we were the most beautiful and wonderful girls in the world. Later when Papa was no longer with us, our father told us the same things. We were blessed from the moment of our births with an abundance of affection. The legacy of that affection stayed with us throughout our lives and fortified us later when we incurred problems because of the Capone name.

After Papa died, Mama Mae never slept another night in their bedroom. She moved all her beautiful things to the bedrooms downstairs. No one else ever slept in the upstairs guest rooms again, either. The kitchen and the big downstairs' porches were where all the living was done. Eventually Mama Mae and her sister and brother-in-law slept in the bedrooms in the guest apartment over the garage. Aunt Muriel, Mama Mae's older sister and her husband, Louis, had moved to Palm Island in the forties after World War II ended. They had been frequent guests at the Island over the years, particularly during the times Mama Mae would travel to visit my grandfather. They oversaw my father's care during those times. In 1945, they gave up their home in Chicago and permanently moved to Florida. On the many nights when Ronnie and I stayed with my grandmother after Papa's death, we slept in the garage guest apartment as well.

Many years later when my grandmother was sitting at her dressing table in the guest quarters and I was brushing her hair, I asked her why we never used the upstairs in the big house anymore. She told me, she wanted to remember the happy times she had there with Papa. "I can never enter that beautiful room now without remembering that night your Papa died there. It is an unbearable memory, so I stay away from it." For her, when Papa died, the house died with him.

Though my grandmother continued to live on Palm Island for many years after Papa died, we never again had a Christmas celebration or birthday party there. Those occasions were held at our house in Miami Shores and later at my father's Miami Beach restaurant.

I was a very little girl when Papa died, and many years have gone by since then, but more than any other of my early memories of times with him, the memory of that night time visit to say good bye and his final words: "I love you, baby girl", have stayed with me throughout my life.

chapter two
MY GRANDMOTHER'S STORIES

IT WAS THE SUMMER OF 1973. I stood watching the planes take off and land at the San Francisco airport wondering if my grandmother's plane would be on time. My grandmother, Mama Mae, had been coming each summer to California for the past several years to visit me, my sisters and our children. I so loved seeing her and always enjoyed hearing stories of her colorful life. Mama Mae always stayed at my house during her visits. My three sisters were working outside their homes, and since I was at home with young children, I got to spend the most time with her.

The airport was crowded as usual, but I had a little time before she was due in and I relished having some time to have a cup of coffee and be alone with my thoughts. Mama Mae was so forthright, and over the years she revealed much of her life to me. I loved our long talks and hearing the stories about her childhood home in Brooklyn, her growing up, and best of all how Papa had come into her life. Not all her stories were happy ones, but they were richly told with such tenderness and passion that I felt as if I was able to go back with her and relive it all, both the good and the bad.

I wondered if I dared tell her about my own life. No, I decided as I sat stirring cream into my coffee. No one in my family knew the darkness I lived with then and I knew that the truth about my marriage would break my grandmother's heart. I would continue the charade. So far I had managed to get away with it. She didn't know that I had been separated from my husband for over a year and had only reconciled with him two weeks before her arrival.

Mama Mae and I had a very special connection. We had often been told that of her granddaughters, I most resembled her and the Coughlin family. More significant than appearance were the similarities in our dispositions. She and I shared a strong religious faith. We were both intensely focused on our roles as mothers, though sometimes overly protective ones, and we were both happy people, who were capable of sweeping almost any unpleasantness under the carpet. We also were both known for our laughter. Regardless of what was going on in our lives we could usually find something to laugh at and both of us had been told by others that our laughter was infectious. The rose-colored glasses, which we both wore, and the ability to laugh despite our heartbreak had been gifts that sustained both of us during difficult times.

As I sat waiting the memories of the past brought tears to my eyes. I had been blessed with a happy childhood and a loving family. I could still remember Papa's and Mama Mae's smiling faces and the long days filled with gentle breezes in their Palm Island paradise. Those were beautiful but distant memories now. The world was no longer a place of happy innocence, even in my own home. "What the hell was I doing in this dark and dangerous marriage?", I asked myself, and then quickly repressed that thought and told myself for the hundredth time I must concentrate on how to make it better and try harder. For now I would focus on putting on a happy face before my grandmother arrived.

I admit it was often a challenge to be upbeat when I contemplated not only my own life, but what was going on around me. Life had been turned upside down for our generation. If I had to use one word to describe the 1970's, it would be "chaos". Television news bombarded us each day with the Watergate scandal and the atrocities of Vietnam. Even in every-day suburbia, traditions and standards that governed mores and expectations had changed seemingly overnight. It was a time of social revolution. The lives of the members of our family, though not usually violent except for mine, in many ways mirrored the turmoil all around us.

I wondered how Mama Mae was coping with all the changes in our family, at least the ones she knew about. It could not have been easy for her when our parents divorced and we moved to California. Daddy still lived in Florida but he had remarried, and so she had a new daughter-in-law to adjust to. He had also finally decided to drop the Capone name and he became Albert Francis or "Sonny" Francis to those close to him. Out of love and loyalty to his father, he had carried the "Capone" name long enough. It was not until many years later and some of the final days of his life that we, his daughters, would learn what it had been like for him to be "Al Capone's only son", but I'll get to that later in the story.

Our mother had resumed her maiden name of Casey and had become a successful business woman after the move to California. She had many friends and a full life, but she never remarried. Mama Mae spent her days living quietly in Hollywood, Florida, far removed from the glamor and luxury of Palm Island, with her older sister Muriel and Muriel's husband Louis Clark. While she never lied about her last name, she was thought of as part of the Clark family, and even her immediate neighbors didn't know they were living next to Al Capone's widow. Two of my sisters and I had rushed into ill-fated early marriages, and so by 1973, my younger sister Barbara was the only member of the family who was still using the Capone name.

Barbara worked for a large electronic company in the San Francisco Bay area. She was one of only two women who, though very young, had climbed the company ladder and found success in a world dominated by white men. It did help that she was almost six feet tall. She was never looked at as a "little woman". She was smart, determined and audacious enough to use the Capone name to advantage. All her co-workers loved her and laughed when she joked with them in meetings that "she would make them an offer they couldn't refuse'. She had the chutzpa to pull it off and never had to endure snide re-marks about being a Capone as Ronnie and I had.

Finally the loud speaker announced that Mama Mae's plane had arrived and I moved toward her gate. I saw her face in the crowd of people disembarking and thought again how lovely she was. Mama Mae was now in her mid-seventies with white hair, but she was slender and her back was straight and she walked with the grace and agility of a much younger woman. She was still in good health and when her eyes caught mine her face broke into her always radiant smile. Oh how good it was to see her, and I prayed that her visit wouldn't be marred by the unpleasantness that often occurred with my husband. It usu-ally didn't happen when there was anyone around to witness it, but he was unpredictable.

We embraced and immediately launched into stories of the family as we headed for the car. She was so looking forward to seeing her three great- grandsons. I sometimes thought my boys, who were close in age and quite rambunctious, took the place of the big noisy family she wished she had with Papa. She always said she wished she could have had a houseful of children. Her face would light up at the mention of them. She often said she could never get enough of playing with them, reading to them and showering them with affection. The boys loved setting up Lego villages populated by little plastic figures and then running their Matchbox cars from one village to another. They would take over the upstairs hallway and bedrooms with their little world of make believe and Mama Mae would be right down there on the floor with them. She had an ageless quality and the boys thought of her as a great playmate. Mama Mae loved being with her family and it is no wonder that we all loved having her around. She was so good natured and always found something to praise in each of us. I one time overheard her saying on the phone to my Aunt, "Oh Muriel, Pat is just like Mama, her floors are so clean you could eat off them," and I was so thrilled I almost cried. She noticed and appreciated everything I did and she never hesitated to say so.

This year Mama Mae's visit to California would be filled with a little more commotion than usual since we were in the process of moving. I never appreciated her good humor more than in the frenetic days during that move. She jumped right in to the packing and most importantly helping with the boys until we could finally get settled.

Mama Mae was an extraordinary woman. She had lived a life of great passion, devastating heartbreak, poverty, followed by lavish wealth and then a very modest existence, not to mention other horrors of which I had no idea at that time. Through it all, her total devotion to family and her deep Catholic faith had sustained her. My grandfather had been the love of her life and when he died, Mama Mae, who was inconsolable, thought that she might not survive, but she did. That steel backbone which had held her up through so many of those desperate times during her marriage did not fail her. That and her unwavering faith enabled her not only to move on with her life, but miraculously to know joy again. Her life was quiet now and her days often filled with prayer and meditation. Her only extravagance was the travel she looked forward to each year, to Chicago and New Jersey to see her younger sisters and a few old friends, and to California to see my sisters and me. Eventually after the birth of her great-grandchildren her visits to California lengthened to several weeks.

I did not find out until many years later that there was a second reason for my grandmother's visits each year to Chicago. My cousin Clairmae told me that each year during her Aunt Mae's stay at their home in Chicago a black sedan would pull up in front of the house. A middle-aged well-dressed man would emerge from the sedan. The doorbell would ring and an envelope with money would be passed. My cousin told me that if the car did not arrive early in her visit, her Aunt Mae would refuse to leave the house for days until the delivery came. Mama Mae who was known for being composed at all times would become quite agitated and express concern that perhaps it wasn't coming. She need not have worried, Tony Accardo, who had taken over Al's business organization "the Outfit" many years before never failed to send someone with her "widow's stipend". Papa had promised she would always be taken care of and she was until close to the end of her life.

Within a couple of weeks of her arrival, our move was completed. It had been hectic, but there were no catastrophes and we were delighted that it was behind us. Mama Mae was a trooper throughout. She never once complained or became impatient during weeks when no one could find their socks or favorite toy.

We settled into the last days of summer and the children went off to school. Many days I would return from dropping off the boys and find her still in her night clothes already folding laundry. She and I would sit down for coffee and the hours would fly by as she regaled me with her wonderful stories of the Roaring Twenties and even earlier times. I would make another pot of coffee, and as we sorted through boxes and folded clothes the stories would continue. Some days we would still be at the table talking when the boys came home from school. Those stories she told me had never been told before and from that visit on each year when she came I would learn more. I especially loved hearing about her childhood and her closeness to her sisters and of course, her life with Papa.

Four Coughlin Sisters 1967 (Muriel and Agnes standing; Claire and Mae seated)

Even though Mama Mae and her sisters were now four white haired ladies in their seventies, when they were together, they were like four young girls laughing and teasing each other. Seeing them together provided a fascinating window into the life Mama Mae had known as a child growing up in the noisy, loving Irish family. Throughout her life, Mama Mae's sisters had always held her up, just as mine had supported me.

As I look back now, I realize that one of the reasons why I was so intrigued and enamored with her stories then was because I had never known a love like she and my grandfather shared. I didn't know what it meant "to feel my knees buckle" as she described her experiences with him or to love someone so intensely that nothing else and no one else on earth mattered but him. Despite all the pain she would suffer later during her marriage, in many ways her relationship with "Papa" sounded like a fairytale romance.

Each year, when she returned to my house, her stories would continue. I would come to understand that my grandmother's memories were sometimes filtered through and enhanced by rose-colored glasses, which she subsequently had passed on to me. This propensity for viewing things thus became a lifetime gift and sometimes a curse that I had to grapple with for many years.

Mama Mae's stories about her childhood home and the early years with my grandfather were told exactly as she remembered them. Like her acute hearing ability, her memory of details was flawless. Her recollections were vivid and the conversations she recounted seemingly were repeated verbatim. I loved her wonderful colorful stories, and of course, had no idea at that time how many of the painful ones were being left out.

In the same fashion, Mama Mae did not know how much I left out of the stories I shared with her. We both tried to concentrate on the good parts of our lives. I told her about my children and how much motherhood meant to me. We laughed about all the dolls she had bought me over the years. In almost every one of my childhood photos, I was holding a doll, some of which were as large as I was, and most of which she had given me. More than any of my sisters, I was always preparing to be a mother. I also told her how much I was enjoying going to college part-time. I had married right after graduating from high school and then worked for two years until my first son was born. My dream of college had been put off, but never abandoned and, in some ways, it meant even more to me now because I had to fight for it. "No, I would definitely leave out the part about the fights my going to college caused", I decided.

I would never tell my grandmother some of the dark secrets I lived with. No one knew that I had been physically and emotionally abused by my husband intermittently throughout the marriage. No, at that time no one knew that part of my story, not my sisters, my parents, my friends; no one knew but my husband and me. It would have broken her heart to hear what I was still going through, so I kept secrets just as she did.

Even though fifty years had elapsed between the memories of her early days of being a homemaker and mine, we happily shared the challenges and pleasures of our domestic lives and laughed at how much some things had not changed. "Just keep it light," I thought. She doesn't need to hear the ugly parts.

Apparently, she thought as I did, "Focus on the happy times." I would not know until many years later how many of her stories were left out or altered. Those stories of fear and betrayal and the devastating heartaches she had endured were not talked about until much later when all her story finally came out.

As I look back now on those conversations I had with my grandmother in the 1970's, my dishonestly shocks me. I sugar-coated everything, mostly to myself. In retrospect, it is hard to imagine that I stayed in that marriage for as long as I did. I was not madly in love with my husband as my grandmother had been with my grandfather, and clearly I did have options then that were not available to a woman in the 1920's. Whether it was my Catholic upbringing, my concern for my children, or just not wanting to admit to anyone what a terrible decision my marriage had been, I lived a lie. Fortunately, I did have options which I belatedly exercised. Divorce was no longer a stigma by the 1970's and the Women's Liberation Movement was making it much easier to have a career and raise a family. A young woman today would find it impossible to believe that rights that they take for granted were impossible for women of my generation. The concept of "domestic violence" and prosecuting a perpetrator did not exist during the years of my abuse. Women in the early 1970's and before had few rights and little control of their destiny.

With all the heartache Papa caused her, would Mama Mae have left her marriage if she had the Women's Liberation Movement and the options I had? The answer is no, she never would have left him. She loved him until the day she died.

chapter three
MAE CAPONE

My grandmother, Mary Josephine Coughlin, was born at her parent's home in Brooklyn, New York, on April 11, 1897. Her parents, Michael and Bridget (nee Gorman) Coughlin, were a beautiful young Irish couple, and Mary Josephine (who would always be called Mae within the family) was their second daughter. Michael and Bridget had immigrated to America from Ireland several years before. They were both from County Cork in southern Ireland and met and married after they arrived in New York, along with so many other young Irish immigrants looking for a better life.

Coughlin home at 117 3rd Place, Brooklyn, NY

Michael had worked as a carpenter in Ireland. He was ambitious and hardworking and felt lucky to have gotten a job as a longshoreman after rather desperate early days in America. It has been reported by some writers that Mae's father worked for the railroad, in construction or in various other positions, but my grandmother told me her father worked on the docks. It was difficult, backbreaking work, but Michael was young and strong and there was no question that longshoremen made more money than any of the other jobs that were open to young immigrants.

The young family grew and in addition to the first two children, Anna Muriel and Mae, it eventually included two sons, Walter and Dennis (always called Danny) and three more daughters: Catherine Claire, Agnes and Veronica. The family grew up in an Irish neighborhood at 117 3rd Place, in Brooklyn. They were a close-knit family, and their lives revolved around St. Mary Star of the Sea Catholic Church, which they regularly attended.

Michael had instilled a love of music and laughter in his children, and the house was often filled with both. Mae's oldest sister, Muriel, would play the old piano in the sparsely furnished front room, and the family was happiest when gathered together in the evenings for stories and songs. Bridget and Michael knew they were fortunate. They had a better life than many other immigrants. Michael's job enabled them to provide a home for their seven children and put simple, good food on the table.

Michael was devoted to Bridget and their family. Unlike so many other hardworking men whose weekly paychecks never made it home after a stop at the pub on payday, Michael brought his pay home to Bridget faithfully every week. Instead of rewarding himself by having a beer with his friends after work, he rushed home to his family. His daughter, Claire, would later tell how her mother, Bridget always spruced up with a clean crisp white apron and pinched color into her cheeks before welcoming her husband at the door. She also managed to save a few pennies from her grocery money for the cost of a pint of beer, which she knew Michael enjoyed. Each Friday, she would send one of her younger children to the pub (called "beer gardens" in those days) with a beer pail to pick up "da's pint" and "Be careful to brush off the foam so you get the full amount and don't you spill a drop on your way home" they were always cautioned. The Coughlins had a happy home. They knew they were lucky and they were thankful.

Abruptly, those happy days came to an end when on April 29, 1913, Michael Coughlin died suddenly after contracting pneumonia. There were no antibiotics in those days and traditional home remedies failed to save him. It happened very quickly. The family was devastated. Michael was only forty years old.

Mae's mother:
Bridget Coughlin

Bridget did not have time to mourn her husband's death, though she never recovered completely from the loss. She had seven children to feed with no life insurance, no social security, and no family from the old country to rely on. The oldest children quit school and went to work immediately in any menial jobs they could find to help support the family. Mae had turned sixteen two weeks before her father died.

The first job Mae got was as a salesgirl in a ladies' clothing shop. As time went by and her confidence grew, she looked for jobs that paid more. Eventually she managed to find a job as a time keeper at United Paper Box Company in Brooklyn. Her paltry salary wasn't much but it was still better than anything she had earned before, and the family needed every cent she could bring in.

She and Muriel and eventually Walter, would turn over everything they earned to their mother each week. It broke Bridget's heart to see how hard they all tried to help and how good they were about it. Without her older children, she and the little ones would be out on the street. The best she could do was to give them back a nickel or two each week. It was not unusual for children to help support their families in those meager times, and at any rate Mae and Muriel said they never minded. They dearly loved their family and were glad to do what they could. Bridget loved all her children but she had a special connection to Mae.

As the years went by Bridget began to realize that Mae was becoming a beautiful young woman. She knew it was only a matter of time before men started noticing how striking she was and she worried about how she would cope when they began to call on her daughter. Bridget knew Mae was smart but she was also inexperienced and totally innocent with men. Bridget missed having her husband's strong shoulder to lean on.

The year was 1918. Mae had turned 21 on April 11. She was five feet six inches tall which was considered tall for a woman of that era. She was slender but full breasted like her mother, and she had gorgeous legs. She had dark brown almost black hair, green eyes and the porcelain complexion so typical of the Irish. She was astute and quickly learned to do any job she was given. Her bosses considered her a conscientious worker and a good Catholic girl. Despite her tendency to

Mae Capone, nee Mary Josephine Coughlin

be reserved, she was proud to be helping out the family, and after a while also enjoyed the camaraderie of the people she worked with. Once she felt comfortable with people she actually became quite witty. She had impeccable manners, was well liked and was fiercely loyal to her friends. Many of the young men at the Box Company vied for her attention and tried to outdo each other to get her to flash that dazzling smile. So far she had kept them all at arms' length.

Mae attended mass at the Catholic Church close to her home regularly with her family. Her faith, her devotion to her family and the simple rhythm of her days in no way prepared her for the man she was about to meet or the turn her life would soon take.

chapter four
AL GROWING UP

LESS THAN A MILE AND a half away from Mae Coughlin's family home in the Irish section of Brooklyn, another family of immigrants was struggling to make a life in the Italian neighborhood. Their worlds were right next to each other, but, in fact, they were vastly different because none of the various immigrant groups intermingled. The Irish, the Italians, the Jews and others kept strictly to themselves.

The Italian family, the Capones, lived in a small apartment at 38 Garfield Place. They had moved several times over the years since the father, Gabriel, and his wife Teresa had first arrived in America from Angri in Southern Italy. Each move was to a slightly improved location and offered more room for their growing family, although none compared to the home of the Coughlins.

Al Capone's family home at 38 Garfield Place, Brooklyn, NY

Gabriel Capone had done better than many immigrants. He knew he would never be wealthy, but he believed that all the sacrifices he and his wife Teresa made would pay off for their children. The Capones had left the poverty and lawlessness of southern Italy in 1895, and now their only desire was to give their children a better life than what they had known. Gabriel was highly intelligent and he quickly became fluent in English. He worked hard and believed like many other immigrants that America was the land where dreams come true. He had no intention of ever returning to Italy, and he could not wait to be able to tell all the family he was an American citizen. He had already filed an application to begin the process to citizenship. After years of struggle, Gabriel now owned his own barbershop on the first floor of the building where the family lived. At that time the majority of barbers in New York were Italians, and Gabriel's business provided just enough of a living to feed his large family. With Teresa's piecemeal sewing jobs and occasional borders, they could just get by.

Like the Coughlins, the Capone family was also struggling to cope with their own loss. In their case it was not the death of a father, but the heartache caused by the disappearance of their first born son, Vincenzo (who was always called James or Jimmy by his brothers). The eldest Capone son had run away from the family as a young teenager in 1908, and for a long time they did not know if he was alive or dead. It was not until many years after his disappearance that they received a short note from him saying that he had joined the circus and was now living in the Midwest. What caused him to run away was not known for almost 40 years. It could have been a row with his father, who was much stricter with his older children, or it could simply have been wanderlust. Whichever it was didn't diminish the feeling of loss within the family.

Gabriel loved all his children, but the one he had highest hopes for was his son, Alphonse. Gabriel told everyone who would listen how smart Al was.

Alphonse Gabriel Capone was born on January 17, 1899, the fourth son, of what would become a family of eight children (seven boys and one daughter.) Even as a little boy, Al showed the greatest promise. He was conscientious and learned quickly. He also was generous and outgoing, and of all the Capone children, he tried the hardest to please his parents, who often agreed that Al did not have a selfish bone in his body. Many of Gabriel's clients at the barber shop noticed and appreciated the attention and respect Al showed his father and them. Often they tipped Al with a few pennies as they left after a shave or a haircut and remarked about what a good boy he was.

When Gabriel took Al with him to the nearby pool hall, Al quickly learned how to shoot pool well enough to compete with the men. Gabriel beamed with pride when other men complemented him on his son. If Al won money playing pool, he promptly gave it to his mother. Both his parents praised his generosity and initiative. Al loved his parents dearly. The more attention and approval they showered on him, the harder Al worked to earn it. He loved feeling important and became increasingly insatiable for the praise of his elders.

One of Gabriel's customers, a man named Johnny Torrio, particularly impressed Al. Johnny was one of the nice men who came into his father's barber shop and gave Al a little tip. He was always well dressed and clearly seemed to be respected by the other clients and Al's father. As Al got older and was out in the neighborhood he frequently saw Johnny Torrio and was soon asked to run errands for the older man. Johnny paid Al as much as five or ten dollars depending on how big the errand was or how long it would take to complete it. Al had never had so much money, and just as he had done when he was younger, he still turned most of it over to his mother.

Al was a smart kid with a happy disposition. He did well enough in school to maintain a B average despite his increasing absences. But by the time he was in sixth grade, his absenteeism was becoming a problem. There are various stories as to why Al dropped out of school, but drop out he did while in sixth grade. Some report that his departure was because of an altercation with a teacher, others say it was because of a beating he received from a principal, and yet it just might have been out of boredom. There is little doubt that he found what was going on outside the classroom to be far more exciting and financially rewarding. A lot of busy men were willing to pay a reliable smart young man generously to relieve them of time-consuming menial tasks.

It was around this same time in Al's life that he became aware of his father's health issues. Whether his father's chest pain was caused by congenital heart problems or by increased smoking and alcohol consumption is not known. What is known is that Teresa Capone told Al when he was eleven years old, "Your father is not doing well, you are the only one I can count on and I need your help." Why Teresa approached her younger son instead of his two older brothers is a question that also has never been answered. Regardless of the reason, her trust in Al was well placed. For the rest of her life, he would be the primary support of her and his family.

Once Al chose not to go back to school, he was free to hustle for as many jobs as he could get, and hustle he did. Al was a big kid, much bigger than other boys his age. Because of his size and his bravado, others often assumed he was older and more confident than he was. Always he succumbed to praise. The more he received, the more he was willing

Al Capone, earliest photograph, approximate age 18

to do to prove his worthiness. He also began to get a reputation as someone who was a tough guy and capable of taking whatever action necessary to achieve his boss's objective. By the time he was a teenager, Al was working full time at United Paper Box Company as well as several hours a week for Frankie

Yale, another prosperous looking, but dangerous, man from his neighborhood. Johnny Torrio had introduced Al to Frankie Yale. Frankie, whose real name was Francesco Ioele, was only six years older than Al, but he was already a man who commanded respect and was widely feared. Laurence Bergreen, who wrote a biography called Capone refers to Yale as "Brooklyn's own Prince of Darkness". Frankie was involved in numerous nefarious albeit profitable businesses.

One of these seedy businesses was on Seaside Walk in Brooklyn's Coney Island, which Johnny named the Harvard Club. The club catered to sailors and other rough customers. Johnny had changed his name from Ioele to Yale and he thought it most amusing to call his bar the Harvard Club. By the time Al was seventeen he was working almost full time at this establishment as a bouncer, a waiter, a bar tender and whatever else Frankie required. As Al moved further and further down the paths of violence and force, both of which he often needed to use to achieve Frankie's goals, he simultaneously moved more and more away from the moral consciousness his parents had tried to instill in him. Like Frankie, Al now also was becoming a dangerous man

If Al had to become a man of violence to financially support his family, and to achieve the admiration he craved, then that is just what he would have to do. One cannot know for sure if Al's family's financial circumstances or his obsession with admiration drove him toward this life of violence, but it is clear from his actions that, as he resorted more frequently to violence, the number and severity of the episodes escalated. He was becoming a more powerful and a more dangerous young man. And yet he still presented a countenance of affability even charm when he chose to.

chapter five
AN AUSPICIOUS MEETING

FROM THE FIRST TIME AL Capone saw Mae Coughlin at the United Paper Box Company where they both worked, he was smitten. It wasn't just that she was a beauty. There is no question that that was part of the attraction, but for Al, she seemed like the realization of an ideal. She had an ethereal quality that set her apart from any woman he had ever encountered and by that time in his young life he had already encountered many. She was the epitome of young Irish womanhood with her porcelain skin and emerald green eyes. He doubted that any Irish woman or her family would ever stand still for an Italian (someone the Irish considered undesirable), even to approach her much less court her. But court her he would, for from the first moment they met he was determined to have her. Al knew that it would be scandalous for an Irish girl to be seen with an Italian boy. Italians were considered "colored" in that era and a marriage, if it occurred at all, were frowned upon as a "mixed marriage". He knew the obstacles he would have to overcome but he wasn't deterred by the thought that Mae was forbidden. If anything, that notion made her an even more desirable prize.

Her head was down and she was preoccupied with the paperwork on her desk when Al first approached her. She did not look up. "Excuse me, miss," he said and she distractedly raised her eyes to see who was interrupting her concentration. Standing in front of Mae was a dark and handsome young man she had never seen before. As she looked at him, Al saw a look of recognition in her beautiful eyes. While they had never met before, she looked at him with such familiarity. Astonishingly, hers was the look of someone who had always known him.

Al paused for a moment and then said, "I am Al Capone". Mae did not hear the rest of his comment. She found herself gazing into the deepest, darkest blue eyes she had ever seen; eyes she felt she had always known. Mae took a moment to get hold of herself and recover her reserved demeanor, but neither of them could ignore the chemistry between them. "I'm sorry, what did you say?" Mae asked. Later she realized that she could never remember what his response had been. What she did remember was an instant awareness that her life had changed and she would never be the same.

Later she would confess to Muriel, that Al Capone was not like anyone else she had ever met. She described him as tall and very good looking, but left out the part about the look they exchanged when their eyes met. Muriel knew that meeting this man was important and wondered why her initial reaction to hearing about him was concern for her sister. As days went by and Muriel realized that Mae and Al were deeply attracted to each other, her concern grew. She would often come home and tell her mother, "Ma, she was talking to that Italian again".

Al had never met anyone like Mae before and certainly had never dated anyone as special. Not that he hadn't known a lot of girls, but they were almost always Italian girls from his neighborhood. There were others as well. Girls who worked at the club where he worked or clubs he often frequented. They were girls of all shapes and types who were eager to please a young man. From a very young age, Al loved women, but all of them paled in comparison to Mae. While Mae was warm and vivacious as some others had been, there were two things that set her apart. Mae radiated a kind of innocent purity and serenity that was unlike anyone else. Al didn't just want to have her, he wanted to marry her. By some miracle Al thought, Mae seemed equally attracted to him.

Al was still working two jobs and giving most of what he earned to his mother. There was little money left to take her on a real date even if her family would allow it. The closest he and Mae came to dating in the early days of their relationship was sitting on the steps of the United Paper Box Co. sharing a can of sardines for lunch.

On one occasion they had been at a dance club that catered to young people, each in the company of others. Mae was with her sister Muriel, and another young woman from work named Louise. Al was standing across the room with his brothers Frank and Ralph when Mae entered the room. He never took his eyes off her. He waited until the girls were sitting down before he approached their table. His eyes lit up and a smile crossed his lips as he made his way across the crowded, noisy room.

Muriel saw him coming before Mae did and she smiled expectantly up at him. He glanced at her, but he only had eyes for Mae. By now he and Mae had spoken a number of times at work and had shared lunch often, but this was the first time he actually spoke to her in front of others in a social setting. He asked her to dance and when he put his arms around her, my grandmother told me she knew she would never want anyone else. He was a wonderful dancer. He was graceful and a strong leader. He held her tenderly, but she was very conscious of the heat and intensity within him. Throughout the dance, he continued to gaze into her eyes and she never once looked away. The music would stop and then start again and yet he never released her. She didn't know how long they danced together, but she told me later she didn't want it ever to stop.

"He was the most remarkable man" she would say years later. "His eyes were like the sea" she said, "sometimes blue green and brilliant and other times gray and stormy". "Whenever he looked at me, I felt like I was the only person in the world."

From that night at the dance club, Al never missed an opportunity to speak to Mae at work. Eventually, he would seek her out especially in the empty stairwells and grab her for a passionate kiss. She told me years later, "My knees would buckle". Neither felt they could get enough of the other. Mae said "almost from the very beginning, they really were madly in love with each other". As weeks went by their passion became more and more intense.

Many years later when she told me these stories about the beginning of their relationship while sitting in my kitchen, she would gaze off into space and her dear lined face would take on the radiance that it surely must have exuded in her youth. "He was the most exciting person I ever knew", she said.

chapter six
AL & MAE

ON ONE OF THE OCCASIONS while visiting me in California my grandmother told me one of the most remarkable stories of all. We had been talking for several hours about her life and she blushingly confessed that my father was conceived in a storage room at the United Paper Box factory. The following is the way she described it.

It was late afternoon at the end of April 1918 and Mae was finishing up at work. She went downstairs to pick up the last of the time cards. Most of the other employees had already left for the day. Al was still there putting something away in a storeroom and, as she walked down the stairs, he looked up at her as if she was an angel descending from heaven. He took her hand and the time cards fell to the floor. He pulled her into the small musty storage room and with the door quickly closed, it was completely dark. Mae had never been with a man before and there was little time to reflect on what was happening. They both were on fire and they grabbed each other as if nothing on earth or heaven could keep them apart. Her urgency was as great as his. With her back pressed to a somewhat dank brick wall, standing up in that storage room, my grandmother lost her virginity. Al was 19 and Mae had just turned 21. Neither of them gave much thought to a possible pregnancy. They just felt being with each other was the best thing that had ever happened to either of them.

As weeks went by and Mae began to suspect she was carrying Al's child, she was terrified. For months, she never told anyone, even Al, about the pregnancy. Finally, by summer, she had to tell Al and her family and quit her job. No one at work could know, even if it meant staying in her room for the rest of her life. Telling Bridget was the hardest thing Mae had ever done. Al, on the other hand, was not remotely upset. His reaction to the news was pure joy.

Al said he wanted to marry her even before she told him about the baby. Within a few days of the time she left her job, Al went to her home to ask for her hand. Mae's mother, Bridget was sweeping the front steps as he approached the house. She looked up with loathing at this dark giant. Al did his best to be respectful and courteous to Bridget, but nothing would sway her. Al pleaded to see Mae and told her mother that he had only good intentions toward her daughter. He said, "All I want is to marry her and take care of her." Bridget hit him repeatedly with the broom and snapped "get off this porch. Until you can give her better than she's got here, you'll never take her from her home".

Mae was standing upstairs at the window and heard everything. She wept as if she would die from the heartbreak. It was the worst day of her life, at least the worst since her beloved father had died a few years before. She begged her mother to reconsider, but to no avail. Bridget loved all her children, but Mae was her treasure, and she had no intention of allowing this "Italian" to take her away.

Many years later when my grandmother was lying on what was to be her deathbed she again revisited the anguish she had felt that day her mother chased my grandfather away. "I'll never forget the despair I felt that day as I saw Al's back when he walked dejectedly away from my house. My mother wept, too", Mae said. Then my grandmother told me something that she said no else had ever heard. She said Bridget told her, "You don't know your own worth. You are special, much more than you realize. I had such great dreams for you. All your sisters and brothers together don't equal the tip of your little finger." No one will ever know if Grandma Bridget really believed what she said that day, but she made Mae believe it. She also convinced her that there was no way Al could provide for her, much less their baby, on the wages he made at the United Paper Box Co. At least here she had a roof over her head and a mother to take care of her during her pregnancy. Bridget did not know about Al's other jobs, but she had heard from Mae that he was helping support his family, and so she assumed he was not in any position to take on additional responsibilities.

More importantly, Bridget detested Al and she told her older daughter Muriel that, "if something happens and there is no baby, I'll never let her marry that Italian." In Bridget's world, a "mixed marriage was as great a sin as an unwed girl's pregnancy." Mae never saw a doctor. For months, she did not leave the house. In time, her mother, Bridget, would deliver the baby and save his life.

As for Al, that afternoon after Bridget threw him off her porch, he was beside himself. He had recently taken a job working as a bartender and bouncer at a Coney Island bar and Frankie Yale's nightspot, the Harvard Inn. Frankie was considered dangerous by many of those he dealt with, but he didn't frighten Al. After doing small jobs for Frankie for a number of years, he was officially on his payroll at the Harvard Inn.

Enraged and desperate after the scene with Bridget, Al headed right to Frankie. Al railed, "What am I going to do? How am I going to try to make things right with Mae, when her mother won't even let me see her?" "She's going to have my kid, and I can't even see her." "I have to find a way to show her mother that I can take care of Mae and make a home for her".

Frankie Yale, a shady and ruthless businessman, had grown to rely on Al, and he did not want to see him lose his head over some girl. He counseled Al, first to calm down and think the situation through. "There is no way Mae's mother would want her daughter to have a kid without being married" Frankie said. The first thing to think about was how he could convince Bridget to let him marry Mae even if he didn't take her immediately out of her family home.

The next thing to think about was how he could start making more money to enable him to support a wife and child. Frankie had a number of business ventures that he was working on and he could always use a smart guy to help out, especially a big guy who was also tough and had already proven his loyalty to him. Frankie had come through again, and Al was beholding to him. He also was determined that he would do whatever he had to do to have Mae for his wife.

Over the coming months, Al was on the go constantly. He was still working at the United Box Company and at Frankie's club as well. Further, anything Frankie needed done on the side, got done. Frankie was very pleased with his protégé and Al's nest egg and his status increased significantly. Al also loved to gamble and he was good at it. In those days, he won far more than he lost. In the meantime, he made sure to pay regular visits to Mae's house to leave flowers or other gifts. Often he was lucky enough to have one of Mae's sisters or brothers answer the door and he could leave the gifts without having to run into Bridget.

Despite the fact that Muriel had told their mother about Mae's chats with "the Italian" early in their relationship, now, she made it clear to Al and Mae that she was on her sister's side. They had always been close and Muriel knew how much Mae was suffering. She was a willing accomplice in passing messages between the two lovers. Bridget's disdain for Al and her determination to keep him away from Mae inflamed the young couple's desire for each other and their resolve to marry with or without Bridget's blessing. Thanks to Muriel's assistance and unbeknown to Bridget, Al and Mae had already begun planning to marry during the Christmas holidays before the birth of their child. Numerous notes had been passed for weeks. Mae was now 21 and she didn't need anyone's permission. The baby, however, had his own timetable, and so he did not wait for their wedding day before making his appearance.

In the early hours of December 4, 1918, Mae's labor began. The baby was early by more than two months. Mae was a healthy young woman and the baby was born without incident, although not without anguish. It was way too soon. Albert "Sonny" Francis Capone came into the world weighing slightly over two pounds. His Irish grandmother wrapped him in a soft wool shawl and put him in a box on the open door of a lighted oven to keep him warm. The doctor later told Mae she had Bridget to thank for her son's survival.

Now that the child was born, Bridget knew she had to relent. She turned in her desperation to the church. Father James Delaney had known the Coughlin family for years. He had officiated at the funeral of Michael Coughlin and knew of the family's devotion. At Bridget's tearful request, the priest agreed that the young couple could wed as soon as possible. On December 30, 1918, at St. Mary Star of the Sea Catholic Church in Brooklyn, New York, Mary Josephine Coughlin and Alphonse Gabriel Capone were scheduled to wed. Their son would be twenty-six days old.

It was late on the night of December 29, 1918. In the Coughlin home, Mae's sisters and brothers had long been asleep. Mae thought she was the only one still awake. She did not realize that her mother Bridget's eyes never closed that night. Her mother was too busy praying and thinking about her husband Michael and what he would have thought about the decisions she had made about their daughter over the last several months. Bridget's heart was heavy. She wept as she thought of her husband's beautiful blue eyes and his strong body and how much she wished she could have had him here to hold her and steady their family. Michael was a strong loving good man and he was someone to rely on when times were difficult. This last year had been more difficult than any Bridget had known since that terrible night five years before when Michael had taken his last breath. Since his death nothing had been the same. Bridget had not felt safe for even one day.

If Michael had been alive, now maybe everything would have been different for all her children. Bridget wept and prayed too that Mae would have a good life with this young Italian who was the father of her child.

In her room on the same floor Mae knew nothing of her mother's despair. She was completely focused on listening and waiting anxiously for every breath her baby son took. He was such a tiny little thing she thought and wondered at the miracle of his survival. Now weeks after his birth, Mae gazed at his precious little face in the small cradle where he slept. As she watched over Sonny, she wondered what her soon-to-be husband was thinking about on this night before they were to be married.

Al had decided to stay at his parents' home the night before their wedding and she missed his presence terribly. Since the day of Sonny's birth, now over three weeks ago, Al had been living at the Coughlin family home. Mae felt so secure when he was close by. Al was young, but mature beyond his years and he was always confident and optimistic about their future. When Al was around, his confidence rubbed off on her. In fact, his good nature and positive attitude rubbed off on her whole family. It was almost impossible to believe that her mother had started to like him. At least she was no longer hostile to him, which was a welcome change from when Al had first introduced himself to her.

Bridget did make it clear that despite their marriage, Mae would not be leaving the family home until Al could prove that he could provide for her. Al and Mae would go along with whatever Bridget required now that they knew they could finally be together.

Tomorrow would make everything better. Mae and Al would be married and nothing would ever again keep them apart. She knew that they could not afford a place of their own just yet, but at least they and their little son would be under the same roof. For now, that was the answer to her prayers. Mae had been brought up as a strict Catholic and her devotion to the church had been the one thing that had sustained her when her father died and in recent months when she had to face bringing her child into the world as an unmarried woman, an unforgivable sin in the world in which she grew up. As she lay there, she thought about all that had changed in the little life she knew before Al came into her world and turned everything on end. She had known him for less than a year and yet it seemed that her life had begun when they met.

Mae smiled when she thought of how proud Al was of their son and over and over he told her, "I am the luckiest man in the world to have this wonderful son and soon a beautiful wife." He said, "as soon as the weather warms up we will buy a buggy and take Sonny for a walk". He could not wait to show off his new family especially to his parents.

As the cold morning light entered her window, Mae finally slept.

A few hours later after a quick breakfast of tea and toast, the Coughlin family stepped outside their door. It was Monday, December 30, 1918, and the frigid morning air singed their delicate Irish skin. It had been one of the coldest winters Bridget could ever remember. The relentless wind made it seem even colder. Her daughters Mae and Muriel huddled together and clung to each other as they walked down the icy sidewalk in front of her and Walter. All held fast to each other trying to avoid slipping.

Father James Delaney had insisted that the wedding take place promptly at 10:00 am after the scheduled morning masses and before a funeral which was scheduled to begin at 11:00 am. Fortunately the church was on Court Street, only a little over two blocks from the Coughlin home.

Bridget was grateful that Father Delaney had relented and agreed to forgo the required announcement of the pending marriage. At that time a Catholic couple's plan to wed was announced at each Sunday mass for three weeks leading up to the marriage. Now that their son had been born only weeks before and then baptized at this same church, no one thought it appropriate to delay Mae and Al's wedding for another three weeks. Finally the day had come.

The lights were still on at the altar when Mae's family quietly entered the church. Candles flickered in front of the Blessed Mother's statue and on some of the side altars. Throughout the church, a handful of the faithful who had stayed after mass whispered Hail Mary's as their rosaries gently moved against the wooden pews. The church was still decorated with Christmas flowers and the smell of the candles and the pine boughs enhanced the beauty of the place. Mae whose stomach had been tight with anxiety, began to relax in the warm familiar setting. She had been coming to this church with her family since she was a little girl and it held memories of happy times as well as sad ones.

Over to the right of the altar in the shadows, Mae could see a handful of people in dark coats standing around a tall broad shouldered man whom she recognized instantly. Al always stood out in a crowd and as he turned to face her, his face broke into a smile that took her breath away. The two families cautiously approached one another and Mae realized that it was probably not a happy occasion for either family. Mae had never met Al's parents. Muriel squeezed her arm as she grinned and said, "Don't worry honey. All will be OK. You're not marrying the family."

Introductions were made quickly and Father Delaney approached them insisting that the wedding take place immediately before the church began to fill up for the funeral service. Their vows and wedding prayers were said within minutes. Later all Mae could think about was the way Al looked at her, his eyes filled with adoration. She had no idea how radiant she appeared until afterward when Muriel told her. She wore a cream colored dress covered with handmade Irish lace. Despite all her mother's disdain for Al and disapproval of the couple, she had worked ever since the baby was born making the dress and surprised Mae with it right after breakfast. It would not be until months later that Bridget would tell Mae about how she had spent the night before the wedding finishing the final stiches on the dress as she cried and prayed.

Once the vows and prayers were spoken, Mae and Al left the church separately, he to escort his parents to their home, and she to her own family home where her sisters and mother had already begun preparations for their wedding meal. Al was to join them shortly at the Coughlin home. Mae whispered "thank you" to the Blessed Mother's statue as she had left the church. Indeed her prayers had been answered.

chapter seven

A FAMILY MAN

FROM THE MOMENT HE WAS born, Albert Francis Capone (always called Sonny), never knew anything but adoration from both of his parents and their extended families. Sonny changed everything. He brought the first real joy to the Coughlin family since the death of Mae's father. Despite Bridget's initial disdain toward Al, she had relented after Sonny's birth and had agreed to allow him to move into the Coughlin house. Even she had to admit that he seemed completely devoted to Mae and their son. Al was always generous with gifts and money and he also had begun providing financial assistance for the rest of the Coughlin family, something that would continue for the rest of his life. In fact, after their marriage, Al became the major source of income for the Coughlin family.

He also brought laughter and a contagious optimism into their house. When Al was there everyone had a good time. For the first time since Mae's father died, Bridget began to be hopeful for her seven children. Maybe at last their struggle to survive would be eased by this big happy affable Italian. Bridget's initial feelings of loathing for Al had been completely replaced by the first signs of actual affection. Bridget acknowledged to Mae that maybe she had been wrong. She began to feel grateful that Al had come into their lives.

Bridget had no idea how Al made his money and didn't ask, but he was clearly becoming more prosperous. Even his clothes reflected that to Bridget's discerning eye. Al had always appeared clean and well groomed, but now his attire was no longer worn looking. She had come to believe that Al was a good provider and maybe a decent man after all.

Al was still devoted to his own family and now that he had moved into Mae's family home he saw himself as a man with an even greater need to make something of himself. He had grown up hungry to be somebody of importance. He wanted to be able to offer all his loved ones more than his father had been able to, and he would do whatever he had to do to make this a reality. By 1919, Al felt that his life was moving in the right direction. He was now a married man, a father, and at work he was considered a man who could be counted on especially when things were tough. Frankie Yale, his boss and mentor, treated him as his right hand man. Yes, Al had what he had always wanted even as a child. He was loved and he was respected.

Al began to earn a well-deserved reputation for being the "go to" person whenever there was a problem either at home or at work. Al was just 20 years old and he was being treated and looked up to as the head of the Capones and to some extent the Coughlin family. Al was not troubled by the extraordinary amount of responsibility foisted upon him. He relished it. The family was everything to him and now that his number of dependents had increased from his own family to include Mae, Sonny and Mae's family, he was all the more determined to do whatever he needed to do to make sure that they never wanted for anything.

As the months went by, Mae began to look forward to finally being able to have a home of her own. Sonny was thriving and she and Al had been talking about getting an apartment nearby. As much as she loved being with her family, it seemed that perhaps the time was right for them to set up their own home. Suddenly in the summer of 1919, their lives were upended. At least for now having a place of their own was not to be.

The entire world was in the midst of the Spanish flu pandemic. It had first been diagnosed in the United States in March 1918. By summer of 1919, one fifth of the world's population, 500 million people, were infected with the deadly virus and thus far over 50 million people worldwide had died of it. One in four Americans had already succumbed. Brooklyn, like most of the East Coast, had been severely impacted although thankfully none of the Capones or Coughlins had been ill. Then toward the end of June, Bridget noticed that she seemed more tired than usual. In the coming days, the whole family realized that Bridget was suffering from more than fatigue. In a little over a week she was gone. Just as the doctors were telling the public that the pandemic was ending, Bridget Coughlin died of Spanish flu on July 8, 1919.

Bridget's death was devastating to the entire family, even Al. Though Al had seen Mae's mother, initially as his nemesis, in the months following the birth of his son, he had grown to respect and care deeply for this tiny little lady with her Irish fury. By the time of her death, Bridget had also grown to care for him.

Mae and her sisters and brothers were still reeling from the loss of their mother when, in late Fall of 1919, shortly before Sonny's first birthday, Al came home and informed Mae that he needed to go out of town on business. By this time, Al had been working for Frankie Yale for over a year and was doing well financially. Mae was terribly distressed and pleaded with him not to go. She could not imagine how the family would get along without his emotional and financial support. He did not elaborate on why he had to leave town so suddenly but he assured her that this was a temporary separation and that he would send for her and Sonny as soon as he could find a place for them. This was all the more alarming to Mae, because the implication was clear. Whether it was sooner or later, they would be leaving Brooklyn and all that was familiar to both of them. In those days, wives seldom questioned their husbands about their work. The man was the breadwinner and whatever he needed to do to support the family would be accommodated. Al was gone the next day. Within a few days, Mae received a phone call from him telling her that he was in Chicago and already looking for an apartment for his young family. He told her he would miss Sonny's first birthday on December 4, but hoped he could soon return to Brooklyn and bring her and Sonny back to settle in Chicago.

Al also told her he was working for Johnny Torrio. It was not until much later, that Al would explain to her that Frankie Yale, had sent him to Chicago at the request of his old friend, Torrio. Torrio had been in Chicago for a number of years and indicated to Yale that he needed a good man he could rely on to help with his own business. Al became that man.

From the moment he arrived in Chicago and renewed his acquaintance with Johnny Torrio, Al knew this place would be a good fit for him. He greatly admired Johnny's demeanor. Johnny had nice manners and while he was capable of angry outbursts, he seemed to have a gentility and finesse that Al had never seen before on the mean streets of New York, especially not from Frankie Yale. Chicago was a new world, and at least initially Al had anonymity. It wasn't long before Johnny knew that this kid from Brooklyn was exactly the person he needed. He was someone who was big and strong and also smart and wily when that was called for. Above all, Al was one hundred percent loyal.

Within a short time Johnny began to rely on Al in a way he had never relied on any of his other men. He trusted Al implicitly and began to groom him to become his assistant. Like Frankie Yale's operation in Brooklyn, the nature of Johnny Torrio's business catered to the baser instincts of men, namely: alcohol, gambling, and girls, in a word, vice. Torrio had a reputation for doing favors for people, but they were always favors with a price tag. He used the considerable income he made to buy off anyone who might impose any restrictions on his enterprise, specifically, law enforcement.

While Frankie Yale had been a tough guy who was like a big brother to Al, Johnny Torrio was a father figure. He was someone a poor kid from the streets would look up to and try to emulate, especially if the kid was smart and ambitious and desperately wanted out of poverty. Johnny opened a door to a life Al never dreamed possible. After a month with Johnny, Al felt secure enough to get serious about finding an apartment for Mae and Sonny. It wouldn't be fancy, but he could afford it and still be able to send money back to the Capones and Coughlins in Brooklyn.

In early January of 1920, Al took the train to Brooklyn to bring his family to Chicago. Mae's joy at being reunited helped her cope with the sadness of leaving her family and the only life she had ever known. It was cold and growing dark when the train bringing Al and his family to Chicago pulled into LaSalle Station. Johnny, true to his word, had sent a car to pick them up and take them to the fourth floor walk-up that was to be their new home. It could have been a mud hut as far as Mae was concerned. All that mattered to her now was that they were under the same roof and would be sharing the same bed.

They settled into their new apartment just a few days before Al's twenty first birthday on January 17, 1920. Al had everything he wanted, his wife, Mae, his son, and a job that provided the money to take care of them and the rest of the family. The seventeenth was also the day Prohibition became the law of the land. It turned out to be quite a birthday present for Al.

chapter eight
CHICAGO
EARLY 1920'S

Mae had been in Chicago for only a couple of weeks, but she was happier than she had ever been. The apartment Al had found

Albert "Sonny" Francis Capone at 1 year old

was small and cold in the height of a Midwest winter, but the weather did not really matter. Nothing mattered except that the family was finally together. After struggling to survive in the first few months of life, Sonny was now a beautiful happy baby. Despite his tiny birth weight, at a little over a year old, he had become quite robust and was a joy to both his parents. With Al away much of the afternoon and evening Sonny had Mae's undivided attention.

She would rock him and sing to him and he would clap his hands and laugh out loud. There were days when she never put him down. How wonderful if every child was loved as unconditionally as this one was. It is no wonder that Sonny grew up to be such a good natured and loving man.

When Al did come home, he always found Mae waiting with open arms. He, too, was happy. He had a beautiful wife, who loved him, a healthy son, and at work, he was highly respected by the other men and appreciated by his boss, Johnny Torrio. The opportunities to make money in Chicago, now that prohibition was the law of the land, seemed boundless. He never discussed any of his business with Mae, and she didn't ask any questions.

As months went by, Al was so busy that his time at home with the family was being cut short. On the nights when he was home it was like a party. They would put little Sonny to bed and after dinner, put a record on the Victrola phonograph Al had just surprised Mae with. He had always been a wonderful dancer and dancing around their little apartment was like being at the best nightclub in the world to Mae. He made everything fun she later told me. Like many highly successful figures, Al had the capacity to compartmentalize his life. He never brought the dark side of doing business, with its ruthlessness and violence, home with him. He was an affectionate husband and devoted father.

Some afternoons they would bundle Sonny up against the cold and take walks with him in his new buggy. Al often accompanied Mae to the market and had begun to teach her how to cook some of his favorite Italian dishes. All the men in Al's family liked to cook and even though Al's mother was in charge of the kitchen in their childhood home, she loved having the boys around and often let them help her at the stove.

Eventually, Al decided to send for his older brother, Ralph, to come to Chicago and help him with the business. Whatever Al wanted to do was all right with Mae, even if their privacy would be affected. Ralph would be sharing the apartment with them temporarily.

Mae's only sadness in her long letters home to her sisters and brothers was that she was not closer to them. She was very much looking forward to the visit to Brooklyn that summer, which Al had promised. She also dreamed of having more children, but so far that hadn't happened. She and Al both came from big families and thought of their siblings as their closest and most trusted friends. Mae wanted that for Sonny, too. Thankfully for her, she had no idea that the dream of a large family would never come true for her. She had no idea what lay ahead with regard to having more children or other aspects of her life or there would have been much greater sadness to talk about in her letters home to her family.

Toward the end of August 1920, Al took Mae shopping at Marshall Field's for a new wardrobe. He wanted their families in Brooklyn to see that his wife was well cared for and that he had become successful. For weeks, Mae had written to her family about their upcoming visit and none of them could wait to be together again. When the day of departure came, Johnny Torrio again sent a car to take them to the train station. Al proudly carried Sonny, and as they departed La Salle Street Station for New York, for their triumphant return to Brooklyn, Mae thought life couldn't get much better.

This carefree trip back to see the family was to be one of the last truly happy gatherings for Al and Mae with their families. Only months after their summertime visit, Al's father, Gabriel died of a massive heart attack. It occurred on November 14, 1920 and he was only 55 years old. Their trip home for the funeral was a time of tears and heartbreak. Then, a little over a year later on December 21, 1921, again heartbreaking news came of Mae's brother Walter's death after a short illness. Not even a year after Walter's death came more sadness. Veronica, Mae's little sister had died on September 25, of bronchial pneumonia. Three members of their families were gone in less than two years. All Al's prosperity could not lessen their sadness. Now when Mae and Al clung to each other, it was not only in passion but in grief.

During these same years, Mae suffered a number of miscarriages and the birth of a second son, who was stillborn. The trauma of this last event left Al shaken with the fear of losing

Mae. As much as they both wanted more children, Al wanted Mae even more. Neither of them had any idea at this point that the syphilis, Al unknowingly carried, was probably the cause of their inability to have more children.

Prohibition had been in effect for over two years. Al was making more and more money, and even while he was fully supporting the two families in Brooklyn, he had managed to put some money aside. He wanted to bring his mother, Teresa, and the rest of family out to Chicago. To do that he would need to buy a home. Al's family had been totally financially dependent upon him since the death of his father. He and Mae started looking for a home that would accommodate all the Capones. In the winter of 1923, Al and Mae purchased a two-family duplex at 7244 South Prairie Avenue in Chicago. The two-story brick building was in a middle class neighborhood and while it was in no way pretentious, it was far superior to the apartments he and Mae had shared earlier in Chicago and to the Capone family residence on Garfield Place in Brooklyn.

Al and Mae shared the three bedroom upstairs apartment with Sonny and whichever of the Coughlin siblings were in town. Mae's sisters came for frequent visits. The lower floor apartment and converted basement would be occupied by the rest of the Capones which included Al's mother, Teresa and his three younger siblings: Mimi, Matty and Mafalda. Frank, Al's older brother had also moved to Chicago and he at that time shared an apartment with Ralph.

After what had been a happy period settling into their new home on Prairie Avenue, Mae was beginning to realize that the private life she shared with Al would never be the same. For instance, it was expected that they would all take their meals together at Al's mother's table downstairs. Gone were the quiet dinners alone and dancing to the Victrola they had so enjoyed in their early days in Chicago.

Mae was a devoted wife and, to her, Al's happiness was more important than her own. Like so many women throughout history, her happiness, came second after her husband and family. She accepted that after five years of marriage, they were no longer starry eyed newlyweds and he was a man of many responsibilities, but how she yearned for those earlier days when she and Sonny had Al all to themselves. Now Al was frequently gone for days at a time. My grandmother told me that anytime she expressed any concerns about family issues or Al's absences, his response was "don't you worry about anything, Daddy will take care of everything". When he did come home, it was always like a holiday celebration with huge meals that his mother prepared and lots of presents and affection for everyone. He would get down on the floor and play with Sonny. In fact, Mama Mae told me Al was so fond of the boy, he would often want to hold him while he was eating his dinner.

Al's older brother, Ralph had been living in Chicago working for Al for a couple of years by 1923. During that period, he frequently returned to New York to visit his son, Ralphie, and wife, Filomena (called Flo). Their marital relationship was always contentious. When Flo received word that Ralph was on his way to New York to bring her and Ralphie to Chicago to live, she abandoned her son and disappeared. Ralph found his young son with the next door neighbors. He took Ralphie back to Chicago and immediately left him to be raised by his grandmother at the Prairie Avenue House.

Once he was settled there, Ralphie was showered with affection by the extended family. Ralphie was only a year older than Sonny and the two were raised more like brothers than cousins. Ralphie never had a really close relationship with his father. Ralph had his own home but he and his son never lived together. Ralph was a cold and distant father figure. He had numerous girlfriends who came and went after his divorce from Flo. A number of them lived with him over the years, but never his son. Ralphie was a handsome boy and very bright. Why both his parents, first his mother, Flo, and then his father, Ralph, who was emotionally unavailable, abandoned him is heartbreaking and hard to fathom. Ralphie was popular and did well in school and college, but he never realized his potential. As an adult, his alcohol addiction and inability to hold down a job eventually led to a failed marriage and suicide. His father was always willing to help him out financially, but apparently was incapable of offering him the emotional support he wanted and deserved. My grandmother later said "the loss of that beautiful young man was just a tragic waste".

Meanwhile, the pattern of the Capone family life at the Prairie Avenue home was happily peaceful for the most part, but Mae was beginning to realize that Al was not just a businessman. She was learning that his life away from home was filled with danger. Mae went to mass almost daily with her mother-in-law at St. Columbanus Church, which was around the corner from their home at Prairie Avenue on East 71st Street. As noted, Teresa and Mae were devout Catholics. One cannot help but wonder if the urgency of these two women's' prayers wasn't an indication of the fear they must have felt for the safety of Al and the rest of the family. While Al did not discuss his activities with them, there were obviously newspaper articles about him available to them. Grandma Teresa never read English, but my grandmother certainly did and her alarm grew. Mae was loving and trusting and wanted to believe that the newspaper was just sensationalizing articles to sell newspapers, but she was no fool. Her rose-colored glasses had helped her maintain some level of innocence, but they didn't blind her to the changes she began to see in her husband.

chapter nine
A DANGEROUS BUSINESS

MAE UNDERSTOOD THAT HAVING HIS family close by was important to Al. Loyalty and commitment to family were the most important values of his life. In Italian families, the tradition of Campanilismo was considered sacrosanct. This tradition dictates that should the father of the family die, it is up to the oldest son to ascend to the role of Patriarch and assume responsibility for the family. Al had three older brothers who were either incapable of or unwilling to assume that responsibility. Vincenzo, Al's oldest brother had run away from the family at the age of 16 and had been heard from only once in the many years that followed. Raffaele (Ralph to the family) was second oldest. As noted earlier, he had followed Al to Chicago the year before his father's death. He was highly intelligent, but he was a cold man who took a backseat to Al, and had for years during their growing up.

Frank (baptized Salvatore when he was born in Brooklyn in 1895), had been the third oldest son, but like Ralph had always deferred to his younger brother. Despite the fact that Al was the fourth oldest son in the family, it was he who would always assume the responsibility of provider for the large family.

Despite Al's determination to keep the family sheltered from the dangers of his life, events in April of 1924 would make that impossible.

Al's brother Frank was killed by the police. Frank was four years older than Al, the tallest and considered by many, the handsomest of the Capone brothers. Frank had eagerly embraced the world of opportunities in Chicago as had Al and Ralph. Like his brothers, he wanted out of the life of poverty and he would take whatever path necessary to accomplish this.

The details of how and why Frank was killed are contradictory. What is known is that late in the afternoon on Election Day, April 1, 1924, in Cicero, Illinois, nine unmarked cars filled with plain-clothed police officers (30 to 40 of them) came to a screeching halt on Cicero Avenue and 22nd Street and a barrage of bullets were fired. The men who were with Frank Capone that day swore he never reached for a gun. The police claimed he fired at them and they shot back in self-defense.

When Al and Ralph later identified Frank's "bullet riddled body" at the morgue, it was apparent that he had been shot dozens of times. A gun with his fingerprints on it was offered into evidence at the official inquest. The court's verdict was self-defense. The family was devastated and Al was outraged. Al perceived Frank's death as an execution and it was a turning point in his life, in that from then on vengeance became a part of his agenda. It was a turning point for Mae as well. She said she never felt completely safe in Chicago after this, even in the seclusion of their home.

On one occasion, Mama Mae told me that she watched cars filled with men drive repeatedly past their home on Prairie Avenue looking for Al. Their guns were clearly visible even in the darkness of night. Al was not at home, but Mae, who was hiding behind a curtain at an upstairs bedroom window observed them and was terrified. She did not know if those men were from rival gangs or the police, and after Frank's death, she didn't trust any of them. During all the years of gang violence in Chicago, families were considered untouchable. Mae had read about killings among rival gangs, but now they were not just stories in a newspaper. The danger Al faced every day was more and more real; the danger in fact was in their own front yard. In the coming years, she would learn to live with this constant fear.

Al had begun spending most of his time in Cicero. He had moved his headquarters from the Four Deuces Saloon in Chicago, which was owned by Johnny Torrio, to the Hawthorne Hotel in Cicero the year before. He also kept rooms at the Metropole Hotel and later the Lexington Hotel in downtown Chicago. He tried to shield Mae and his family from the escalating threat of violence. He and Johnny Torrio continued calling themselves businessmen. They claimed they wanted to avoid trouble and in most instances paying people off had worked. Al often complained that as far as he was concerned he was simply providing a service by supplying alcohol to hardworking people. Al would add, "This is a free country, and I am just doing business like any other businessman;" and "Don't people have the right to have a drink after a hard day?" Al told those closest to him, "The hypocrites who are coming after me and yelling the loudest are my best customers".

During these years of Al's growing dominance in Chicago, there were numerous attempts on his life by other gang members. Just staying alive had become a full time job for him. In what was later considered the first biography of Al Capone, written in 1930, the author, Fred Pasley claimed that "Al was the most-shot-at man in America." Al continued to state publicly, "there's plenty to go around for all of us." Clearly, the rival gangs thought he was getting too big a piece of the pie.

When it came to other gang leaders, compromise was sought and agreements were made. Unfortunately, "honor among thieves" could not be depended upon. Some people gave their word in literal "blood oaths" and then broke them. When this happened, revenge was swift. Retribution led to retribution and by 1925, all of Chicago reeled from the ongoing violence.

Just after Christmas, in January 1925, Johnny Torrio was shot five times and left for dead in front of his home as his wife watched in horror. When Al heard about this, he was enraged and swore vengeance. There would be no peace until the responsible parties were dealt with. The two men who had been identified by witnesses as involved in the shooting were Hymie Weiss and George "Bugs" Moran. The police arrested both men and took them to the hospital to be identified by Torrio and his wife. Torrio, to the surprise of his doctors, had miraculously survived the assassination attempt and was slowly recovering. Neither he nor his wife would identify the shooters.

Shortly after the near fatal attack and still frail, Torrio appeared in court and plead guilty to a charge of operating a brewery. As always, Torio's timing was impeccable and his wealth and contacts assured his comfort even while incarcerated. He was sentenced to nine months in jail, a sentence that precluded further attempts on his life. At least temporarily, he would be kept safe while recovering. He served his time in his luxuriously appointed jail cell with the best protection money could buy. As soon as he was released, he and his wife left Chicago for an extended trip to Italy leaving the business in Al's control. Torrio knew that gang wars were getting worse and he no longer had the stomach for it.

There was no doubt in Torrio's mind that Al would have to deal with running their highly organized business in a state of open gang warfare. Al, too, for the first time since coming to Chicago, began talking with the family about settling some old scores and then getting out.

Within three years, Al bought the house on Palm Island in Miami Beach, and began what he thought would be a gradual withdrawal from his role in Chicago. Unfortunately, the ties that bound him were far more difficult to break and subsequent events led to totally unforeseen consequences that neither he nor Mae could have imagined.

Another big change in Mae's life was that there were sometimes weeks when Al did not come home at all. Since 1923, shortly after the family moved to the Prairie Avenue home, Al had spent most of his time at the Hawthorne Hotel in Cicero. Initially, he had indicated that it was to assure the family security and to some extent that was accurate. Mae had no way of knowing at that time, though, that it also provided Al with the privacy he needed to conduct his business operations as well as his new flamboyant personal life.

When he did come home, usually each Sunday, it was with lavish gifts and the same loving and affectionate manner he had always shown her. He was a passionate man and their love life, while now sporadic was nonetheless exciting and satisfying. Al always treated Mae with great respect and told her she was the most wonderful wife in the world. He still acted when he was with her like she was the only woman he ever wanted. Unfortunately, Al's insatiable sexual desire was no longer just for her. When he was away from home, he had another life. From his perspective, whatever happened in that other life had nothing to do with Mae. He still thought of himself as a loving and devoted husband.

Mama Mae told me she couldn't remember what first made her aware that there were other women in Al's life. It might have been some offhand comment one of his brothers made. Like most loving spouses, she initially tried to dismiss this ugly suspicion. As months went by, the sick feeling in her stomach became a constant ache.

Finally, she could not stand not knowing. She asked her brother-in-law to drive her on an errand. Once in the car, she insisted that she was to meet Al at the Hawthorne Inn.

When she arrived at the hotel, she approached Al's suite and was met by armed bodyguards, who attempted to block her entry. She, for the first time in her life with Al, lost her temper and shouted at the men to, "get out of my way." When they tried to stop her, she shouted again, "what do you think Al will say, when I tell them how you treated me?" The men knew that Al adored Mae and was very protective of her regardless of how many young women might parade in and out of his quarters. There was no way they wanted to incur his anger so they parted and let her through.

The commotion outside his door did not go unnoticed. When Al heard Mae's voice, he jumped up and told the half-naked girl to grab her things and leave by the only possible exit, the fire escape. The most feared man in America, who wasn't afraid of anyone, was scared to death of Mae's catching him with another woman. Mae might have been innocent and trusting, but she was no fool. She knew what was going on and she flew into a rage that terrified him. When Mae described this terrible row to me many years later while sitting in my kitchen, she actually laughed. She said it was the only time in her life when she saw fear on Al's face.

She did not hear from Al for days after this scene. Finally, when he did appear, he was just as loving and affectionate as always. His mother prepared a huge feast as she always did to welcome him home. If anyone in the family knew about what had happened, they never mentioned it. Mae, too, behaved congenially as if nothing had changed. Finally, when they went upstairs, she took Sonny into his room and Al started to follow. She turned on him like a tigress, and hissed at him, "don't you dare enter this room with my son." She didn't elaborate on the rest of her diatribe. Suffice it to say, I don't think my grandfather would ever have stood for that kind of berating from anyone else on earth. Finally, when her fury was spent,

Al looked at her and without saying a word, he spat across the threshold on to the floor of the room and walked away.

A few days later, a package was delivered for Mae. When she opened it in the privacy of her own room, she saw a magnificent diamond and platinum bracelet with a loving apology and promise of his undying devotion to her. When Al next appeared, nothing more was said. She did what she would grow to do over and over again in her life. She swept her heartache under the rug and moved on. He was back, and that was all that mattered to her.

Only one other time, did Mae say that her temper flared. A few years after that first incident, Mae was standing in her mother-in-law's kitchen and from one of the bedrooms in the basement she overheard one of Al's men make reference to Al's new young blond companion. This situation regarding the blond was not only heartbreaking and a breach of his promises, but was humiliating. Everyone seemed to know about it, but Mae.

When Al came home for Sunday dinner with the family that weekend in his brand new Cadillac, she retaliated in the only way she could. It was early afternoon when Al arrived with his driver and two bodyguards. After greeting Mae, Sonny and all the family, Al called to his men to come in and join them for one of his mother's feasts. Mae quietly slipped out the back door and hurried around to the front of the house where the new car was parked.

Mae had never learned to drive, but she had watched the sequence of steps that her drivers used. She told me she was shaking like a leaf, mainly because she wasn't sure she could get the car started. She almost bit through her lip as she turned the key and heard the motor start. She wasn't sure which pedal to step on, but somehow she chose the right one. As she pressed down on the clutch pedal, she pushed the gear shift with all her might and then stomped on the gas pedal as hard as she could. The car leapt forward and smashed into the side of the garage just as Al's bodyguard came flying through the front door of the house.

Al was right behind him and when he saw Mae slumped over the steering wheel, he feared the worst. As he threw open the door afraid that she might be injured or even dead, he saw that she could barely lift up her head. As he gently reached for her, realizing that her body was convulsing, she turned and he saw her mouth wide open, not in fear or pain but in a paroxysm of laughter. She laughed so hard she couldn't get her breath. She actually thought she might kill herself laughing and she didn't care. "That's what I think of you, Mr. Al Capone, Big shot," she whispered under her breath. Al didn't say a word. The car was fixed. There was little more said about the blond. And my grandmother went to the beauty salon that week and had her beautiful dark hair bleached platinum.

In the years to come, there were other instances when Mae was quite sure he was seeing other women. Somehow despite her heartache and anger, she managed to reconcile herself to the fact that whoever he might be with, he always came back to her. She never questioned his love for her or his devotion to their son. She also told me, "there was never a time they went to bed, that he didn't reach for her". She knew

Mae and Al Capone at Sunday dinner on Prairie Avenue, Chicago 1926

she would not leave him and so the only course of action was to close the door on his infidelities just as she had managed to do with other even darker aspects of his behavior.

She put on her special rose colored myopic glasses that helped obscure the dangerous path Al had chosen. She tried to focus only on the warm loving side of her husband. She knew that was the only way she could survive, and by God, she would survive.

As the twenties wore on, there were many terrible days to come for Mae: days when she learned of assassination attempts on Al's life; days when police would come looking for him; and weeks when he would disappear and she would just have to wait for word of him. Through it all she never stopped loving him and she never stopped praying for him and his immortal soul.

Apparently, from Al's letters to Mae in years to come and from what he told Sonny, he never stopped loving her either. For Al, who had been a young man in his twenties at the height of his power, other women were merely amusements and distractions in the midst of a dangerous life. The only woman who ever had his heart was Mae.

Years later, when I was told these stories by my grandmother, those about the other women were the hardest for me to

Al and Sonny Capone at Hot Springs, Arkansas 1925

fathom. Is it possible to love someone so much that you could close your eyes to their repeated betrayal? It took even longer for me to realize that his unfaithfulness was only part of what she had closed her eyes to. Apparently, my grandmother had learned to compartmentalize her heartbreak and disillusion as proficiently as my grandfather had the atrocious aspects of his own life many years before.

My grandmother told me that there were occasional respites from the fear and agony. Sometimes Al would take the whole family to Hot

Springs, Arkansas, or Florida for vacations, and at these times, he seemed much like the sweet boy she had fallen in love with. When she watched Al play with Sonny and heard their laughter, Mae's heart was overwhelmed with tenderness.

Finally, in 1928, Al announced he wanted to move Mae and Sonny to Florida with him. He had seen a place on an island just off Miami Beach and it looked like paradise.

chapter ten
FLORIDA 1928

FLORIDA IN 1928 WAS A tropical paradise. After living in Brooklyn and then Chicago with their harsh winters, Al and Mae found that Florida's warm ocean breezes, year-round sunshine and gently swaying palm trees made Miami Beach seem like heaven. Al was at the top of his game. It was purported that his business enterprises generated over a hundred million dollars a year. He had managed to take control of the Torrio operation in Chicago despite ongoing disputes with rival gangs. Al usually tried to emulate Torrio, and whenever possible negotiate agreements with his competitors rather than resorting to violence. He was often heard saying "there is enough to go around, let's not be greedy". Al also believed that when negotiations broke down or people broke their word, he had enough muscle to insure that he had the final say.

On the other hand, there was no question in the minds of his Chicago rivals that Al Capone had the biggest piece of the action, and they were willing to fight to challenge his dominance. Numerous attempts were made to "get Capone". Whenever one of Al's men or one of his friends was hit, retaliation would occur, and violence begat more violence.

Unfortunately, over the four years since Frank Capone had been killed and the almost fatal attack on Johnny Torrio, violence had escalated beyond any one's worst nightmares. The police called this ongoing bloodbath in Chicago, the "Beer Wars".

That was part of the reason for Al's move to Florida: to escape the constant violence or threat of violence for himself and those closest to him. Not that Mae or Sonny were in any eminent danger in Chicago, but accidents did happen, even though most of the gangsters had spared the families.

Throughout the entire era of prohibition and gang warfare (1920 to 1933) several hundred killings had occurred in the Chicago area according to news accounts but there were no incidents of women and children being targeted. Al knew he had many enemies and countless attacks had been made on him over the years. He was a man who had chosen a dangerous way of life. He would take whatever came his way, but he wanted Mae and Sonny removed from the darkness of his life in Chicago and the bloodshed.

For her part, Mae hoped this move to Florida would be a wonderful new beginning for all of them. Al bought the house and put it in Mae's name. He then immediately set about building a huge swimming pool with three diving boards. He built a two story pool house. He also had the boat docks enlarged to accommodate multiple boats. The dock was on Biscayne Bay with access to the Atlantic Ocean. As soon as the building was completed he bought a beautiful teak speedboat which he named the *Sonny and Ralphie*.

Sonny and Ralphie had grown up together and Al anticipated many happy times on that boat for both of them. Al then sent Mae on a shopping spree to furnish the house as lavishly as she wished.

Mae was overjoyed. It was 1928, the country was booming; Sonny was healthy and a joy to both of them and she believed finally now in this beautiful new home there would be some peace in their lives. Sonny was thriving in this warm climate and they both loved having more time with Al. Also, Mae's younger brother, Danny, had moved to Florida and her sister,

Muriel with her husband, Louis, would join them often as well. The house in Florida could accommodate lots of visitors.

Ever since she had married, Mae told me she thought being with Al was like being at a party. Now, with Al in Florida for weeks at a time, there were real parties with sometimes hundreds of guests. Al loved having a house full of friends and family. Mae's shyness was a thing of the past. She dressed elegantly now and presided over dinner parties as if she had been doing it all her life.

Mae said a quiet evening was when there were fewer than thirty for dinner. It was a time of extravagance and lavish life-styles for those who could afford it. In Miami Beach in 1928 and 1929, there were many people who could afford it.

As months went by, Mae began to believe that they would finally have the family life she had prayed for. They were never able to have more children, but they had Sonny and he was the joy of their lives. He was every bit as brilliant and vibrant as Al, but he had never been hungry and he had never known fear.

"Sonny" Capone 1928

He was a child who had grown up in a world of love and privilege, but he did not have a hint of entitlement or selfishness. From an early age, Sonny's generosity and cheerful disposition reminded Mae of Al. Unlike Al, however, there seemed no capacity for ferocity. For this, Mae would be eternally grateful. It would be unbearable to live in fear of losing Sonny as she did of Al. Al never talked about the danger he faced almost every day, but she knew it had become his constant companion.

She far preferred thinking about how lucky she and Al were to have such a wonderful son. After Sonny's premature birth and then a severe mastoid infection requiring life threatening surgery, he had grown to be a healthy and happy child. He would always be hearing impaired as a result of the mastoiditis, but there were new hearing devices available, and his diminished hearing never seemed to incapacitate him.

Mae would never forget the terror she felt when she thought she might lose him in 1925. It had begun as a cold, but then Sonny got very sick very quickly as children often do. One minute he was fine and playing and the next, feverish and pale. The doctor who examined him had a very concerned expression on his face and said Sonny would have to be admitted to the hospital immediately.

My father, Sonny, recounted the following story to me many years later. He said, he had been admitted to the hospital and while he couldn't remember all the details, knew that he had been in hospital for at least a few days and whatever was wrong with him was serious. He knew that by the look on his mother's face. She never left his side and he had never seen such fear in her big green eyes before.

Finally, his mother had been sent home and his father was sitting next to his hospital bed holding his hand and singing a little song to him. Al looked scared too and that was not a look Sonny had ever seen before on his father's face. The doctor entered the room and Al stood to confer with him. Whatever the doctor was explaining to my grandfather must have been very upsetting because Sonny said that his father became very agitated.

All of a sudden, Al turned and picked up a large brief case he had set beside Sonny's bed. Al opened the bag and dumped the contents on the hospital bed where Sonny was lying. My father said the bed was covered with packs of money. Papa turned to the doctor and said, "Don't let my boy die". "If this is not enough money, I'll bring more". The next thing Sonny remembered and recounted was something that occurred what seemed like a few days later. Sonny was still in the hospital bed, but was no longer in pain and was feeling a lot stronger. Again, my grandmother had been taken home and Papa was in the room talking with the doctor. At last, Al picked up the phone in the room and called home. He asked for Mae. When my grandmother tearfully came to the phone, he asked, "Maggie, do we have any beer in the house?" My grandmother said, "yes of course." Al said, "Open it all, Jiggy is going to be O. K."

Sonny loved to read adventure stories and had become an excellent student. He had to be careful about not getting water in his ears, so water sports were very limited, but he excelled and thoroughly enjoyed almost all other sports including golf, football, tennis, riding horses, even roller skating. Also, like his father, he loved music, and throughout his life, was always considered an excellent singer and dance partner.

Those years were some of the happiest years Mae had known since the early days of their marriage when Al first brought her and Sonny to Chicago. They lived a very protected life on the island and were insulated from the financial troubles that many were having just before the beginning of 1930. When Mae did travel north to see her family in Brooklyn or the Capones in Chicago, she was horrified at the poverty and desperation of many Americans. Al was equally troubled, especially when it became apparent that so many children were going hungry.

He was the first individual citizen to open a soup kitchen to feed the poor. This kitchen served food to over three thousand people in Chicago the first day alone. My father told me that he remembered once being with Al in a private dining room in Chicago for a banquet with a large group of associates. He said, as the dinner was being served, Al looked out through the window and saw the faces of countless newsboys peering hungrily in at the laden table.

He shouted to the waiters, "get those kids in here right now and feed them". My father said, he remembered feeling such pride that his father wanted to make sure the children were fed before he would sit down to his own dinner.

My father also told me that he had seen his father give newspaper boys a hundred dollar tip on numerous occasions always, with the instructions, "go right home and give that money to your mother".

There was no question that Al lived lavishly, but there were countless stories also told of his great generosity. Mae told me many years later that throughout the early years of the Depression money was poured from Al's coffers into feeding the hungry. Even when it appeared their lives were being turned upside down by police, the courts, in fact, the full weight of the Federal government, Al still directed the soup kitchen to be stocked to serve the poor.

chapter eleven
GROWING TREPIDATION

Mae loved Florida. Even more, she loved their lives in Florida. During the time between 1928 when they first moved to Palm Island and early 1929, Mae reveled in the peace of those sunny days and she repeatedly told her family, "all was grand". As time went by, however, she began to feel a growing anxiety.

She told me that she was not sure why she had a sense of foreboding. She said she kept thinking it was just her Irish melancholy or superstition. She wondered if things in her life seemed too good to be true. She said she tried desperately to put those thoughts out of her mind, but when Al was out of town on business and Sonny was busy with his lessons, there were moments of reflection, when Mae felt a sick fear come over her. She had the feeling that at any moment "the other shoe would fall". Mae had become very adept at living in denial. Even if she had known of this defense mechanism, she never would have recognized it in herself. She scolded herself for just being a pessimist and worrying too much. She tried as best she could to sweep her anxiety under the rug and to always present a smiling face. Al often told her that was one of the things he loved most about her that she was such a happy woman.

As Al's name was mentioned more and more often in the newspapers during 1929, Mae began to realize there was a reason for her trepidation. Weekly, there were headlines and stories of violence and often Al was the alleged perpetrator or mastermind. Worst of all was the unspeakable horror of the St Valentines' Day Massacre which was splashed across every newspaper, and the claim that Al was responsible for it. Mae tried to keep newspapers out of Sonny's view, but he was in school now and so likely heard about the accusations from other classmates. Until February 14, 1929, the citizenry of Chicago seemed ambivalent about Al. Many actually thought of him as a tough, but pretty great guy who furnished their booze and accommodated their other vices. They seemed not to mind that he was "getting away with breaking the law and no one appeared able to stop him." At any rate they were willing to look the other way when skirmishes occurred between rival gangs, as did the police and judges (many of whom were on the Capone payroll or at the very least were regular customers of his). Bootlegging was a dirty business and that sometimes included violence, especially when one gang broke the rules and tried to encroach on another's territory. But after the vicious St. Valentine's Day murders of seven members of the George "Bugs" Moran rival gang, no one would look the other way again.

Al, who had just turned thirty years old, was considered the most famous bootlegger in the world and the most powerful crime figure in Chicago. Many people knew of the animosity between the Capone gang members and those who worked for George "Bugs" Moran. It was speculated that Al had planned and overseen the massacre even though he was not in Chicago at the time of the murders. Meanwhile in Florida, Al seemed to take it all in stride and went on about his business. If he felt a growing anxiety, he never spoke of it or at least he never spoke of it to Mae.

In April of 1929, Al invited some of his friends from the old days in New York down to Palm Island to enjoy the sunshine and the spectacular pool he had just built. All the guys swam and went fishing and had a ball. Al particularly enjoyed taking home movies of all of them with his new toy, a moving picture camera. Those home movies still exist. While the guys were there, including Al's old friend, Charles "Lucky" Luciano, they also talked about scheduling a meeting of all the big bosses to try to bring about a truce in Chicago. "Lucky" told Al that Johnny Torrio, who was home from Italy and now living in New York had specifically requested this meeting.

Al would never refuse a request from Torrio, his old partner.

Charlie "Lucky" Luciano visiting at Palm Island in 1929

At the end of May 1929, shortly after the visit from Luciano, Al announced to Mae he would be taking a short business trip. When he saw the look of anxiety on her face, he assured her it had nothing to do with the recent events in Chicago and he wouldn't be gone long. Mae still worried. In fact any time he was away she was afraid for him. She was aware that numerous attempts had been made on Al's life in Chicago and she believed that Florida was the only place where he was safe.

Al Capone strolling with friends in Atlantic City, NJ 1929

Al and a number of big time gang bosses were to attend this gathering in Atlantic City. Mae was not told about the trip until the day before Al was supposed to leave. He did not elaborate about the planned meeting, but he assured her that he would only be in Atlantic City for a few days. As always, Mae did not ask a lot of questions. The one thing she told me years later that she did remember about that trip was Al's statement that, "we have to get things to quiet down". He was looking forward to seeing some of his old friends and hoping that with Torrio's assistance, there could be a truce with his enemies in Chicago. It was time to bring an end to all the bloodshed of the last few years. He also told Mae, he wanted to stay in Florida permanently and leave the operations in Chicago in somebody else's hands, just as Torrio had done years ago with him. He said things were just getting too hot in Chicago and he hoped he could follow Johnny Torrio's example and retire so they could enjoy their life in Florida. Mae was overjoyed.

Apparently, the meeting in Atlantic City went pretty well and after several days of discussion, everyone agreed to Torrio's proposed truce. There were, nonetheless, still a lot of bitter feelings amongst the various gangs. Al had learned over the years not to be too trusting and he knew he could never turn his back on some of the men at that meeting. He would proceed with caution and he believed Johnny's parting suggestion to him might be the answer.

On his way home from Atlantic City, he and his bodyguard, Frankie Rio, took the train from New York to Philadelphia and intended to catch the connecting train that afternoon to Chicago. They claimed that they arrived in Philadelphia late and found that they had missed their connecting train to Chicago. They booked a later train and with a couple of hours to wait decided to head into a nearby movie theater to kill time. Upon leaving the theater, they were arrested by the police and both were charged with carrying loaded weapons illegally. Al had been arrested on a number of other occasions, but he had always been released. This time he was booked, tried and sentenced to one year in prison within 24 hours of the arrest for carrying a concealed weapon.

For the first time in his life, Al Capone was convicted. He would serve time in Eastern State Penitentiary in Pennsylvania. Many were skeptical about this conviction. Some even implied that Al had deliberately gotten himself put away to allow for a "cooling off period" in Chicago.

When Mae learned of Al's conviction, she was shattered. "The other shoe had dropped." She took Sonny to Chicago and as quickly as possible, proceeded with Al's mother, Teresa, and his brother, Ralph, to see Al in Philadelphia. Mae told me seeing her husband in that awful place was one of the worst days of her life. She said she would never believe what some people said about Al arranging to be deliberately incarcerated. She didn't realize that Al was doing exactly the same thing that Johnny Torrio had done in 1925 after a near fatal attack on his own life. Johnny had served a nine-month sentence in jail which might have saved his life or at least prevented another attempt on it. Johnny believed that "cooling off period" had saved him and he thought that it might be worthwhile for Al to do the same thing.

Johnny knew all about the repeated attempts on Al's life and he didn't want anything to happen to him. Despite Mae's insistence to the contrary, it appears that the speculation about Al participating in his own arrest and incarceration was accurate. Though Al would be given privileges that other inmates could only dream of, he was still behind bars for the first time in his life. As always, Al put on a big smile and sounded optimistic when his family arrived to visit him. He knew Mae and his mother were devastated, and he certainly wouldn't make it any harder on them by complaining or acting "down in the mouth". "This was a lousy break, but he'd find a way to make the best of it" he told Mae.

Al had asked the warden and was given permission to have some of his own furnishings brought in. If he had to spend several months in prison, he wanted his own things around him, and he knew he could count on Mae to make those arrangements. She would do anything she could to make him comfortable. Soon he was having special meals brought in and running his business from his cell. Hardly what one would expect in prison, but despite some luxuries, there is no doubt that he spent ten months of his life in prison. Al tried to reassure Mae that at least he didn't have to worry about being shot in prison, and it would give him some time to figure out how to turn the business over to someone he could trust. He also had to figure out how to best deal with the new Federal investigations that were going on and as always, he held on to his optimism.

Al's mother, Teresa, sobbed and sobbed when she saw him on that first visit, Mae told me she would never let on how broken she herself felt. She thought that if Al saw her despair, it might break him and he needed the reassurance of her smiling face. She thought he could face anything for himself, but he needed to know that she and Sonny were O. K. Mae's indomitable spirit held. She walked into that prison with a straight back and an energetic positive gait. If Al could take this on the chin and keep smiling, so would she. At least she would hold herself together until after the visit, and then she would have many sleepless nights to cry when only God could see her tears and hear her prayers for Al's safety. The coming months would pass very slowly for her and Sonny on their return to the beautiful island home. It would not be until many years later that Al would finally tell Mae the truth about Philadelphia and about everything else and those were some of the stories she would share with me years later over coffee in my kitchen.

Over the months while Al was away in 1929 and 1930, there were more newspaper stories that filled Mae with terror. When she visited Al and mentioned her concerns, he dismissed them with such nonchalance that Mae let herself believe that perhaps she was overreacting to the stories. Except for Philadelphia, Al had always managed to avoid serious problems with the law and maybe this new threat regarding Federal investigations would be short lived. That was not to be.

chapter twelve
THE THIRTIES AND
THE TERRIBLE TIMES...

AL HAD A STRONG BUSINESS mind and he kept most of his financial records in his head. There was no way, however, with the size of his business and the necessity to delegate some of his operations to others that all who worked for him could do the same. He was extremely careful about having only his most trusted associates involved in his sparse record keeping. He rightly believed that the less that was written down, the less chance anyone would have of finding out the scope of his activities and the income that was being generated. Nevertheless, the IRS had gotten their hands on a ledger/account book from one of the big Cicero gambling places. Al was unaware of this.

When Al was released from Eastern State Penitentiary on March 17, 1930, his first order of business was to meet with attorneys to discuss the best approach to dealing with the income tax evasion case the IRS was preparing. The attorneys told Al that the weight of the Federal government was being thrown into mounting a full scale investigation of Al's business. They had every intention of bringing charges on the man who had been identified by the Chicago Crime Commission as Public Enemy No. 1. If they couldn't get him for what they believed were his myriad crimes of bootlegging and violence, they would go after him for tax violations. That was the new twist in the FBI's investigations. Instead of looking at how Al made his money, the focus now was on how much money was he really making and whether he was filing appropriate income tax statements. It is somewhat ironic that just that year, Al's picture was on the cover of Time Magazine and he was referred to as "the John D. Rockefeller of the underworld."

Al Capone was now 31 years old. He had with courage, determination, ingenuity and ruthlessness raised himself and his family from obscurity and poverty in Brooklyn to a place in history. His name was recognized all over the country and eventually would be recognized all over the world. Had he sometimes used violent means to achieve his goals? Absolutely, he had. Along the way he had broken many laws, but he had also taken care of his family, fed the hungry, protected his friends and built an empire. From his own biased perspective, he was no different from Rockefeller or Vanderbilt or any other highly successful American. He had succeeded beyond anything he could have imagined. He had faced tough times before and he would face them again.

He wasn't terribly concerned about the possible new tax charges against him or at least he never let on even to his brothers and friends that he was concerned. All those closest to him, including his attorneys, were very concerned. When they expressed their fears, he brushed them aside. He had managed to buy his way out of any previous problems he had encountered. He had influential friends who were lawyers, judges and cops. He did not believe this time would be any different. But it was.

Al might have had a lot of influential friends, many of whom were on his payroll; but he also had a number of influential enemies. No one rises as quickly to the heights he had achieved without accumulating mortal enemies. In addition to which, a lot of good people, moral public servants including President Herbert Hoover, were disgusted with gangland violence and the total disregard for the laws prohibiting the sale of alcohol. Al Capone's name would always be synonymous with both.

President Hoover, who was a conservative Republican and a Quaker, had been elected in 1928. He began his presidency in March of 1929. It was the end of the "roaring twenties", "the jazz age". A lot of people were riding on what they thought was an endless high, largely driven by Wall Street euphoria and illicit booze. American economy and optimism were also at an all-time high. Only months into Hoover's term as 31st president, the economic bubble burst. Hoover tried desperately, but unsuccessfully, to stem the downward spiral of the country into the Great Depression.

Despite Hoover's inability to effectively turn the economy around, there was another matter that he believed he could do something about: the flagrant violations of the laws regarding prohibition. By 1930, the very unpopular law had been in effect for a decade and was being ignored as more and more people learned to circumvent the laws preventing the purchase of alcohol. It was not illegal to drink; it was illegal to make, transport or purchase alcohol. Al Capone and his associates, along with many other canny entrepreneurs, made the "stuff", imported it and delivered it to anyone who wanted it, including some of the same people who were hypocritically condemning bootlegging. Two of Al's statements addressed this: "All I ever did was sell beer and whiskey to our best people. All I ever did was to supply a demand that was pretty popular." Another time he said, "They call Al Capone a bootlegger. Yes, it is bootlegging while it's on the trucks, but when your host at the club, in the locker room, or on the Gold Coast hands it to you on a silver tray, it's hospitality."

As the storm of legal pressure built against Al, an incident occurred that demonstrated the ambivalence of many of the American people about bringing him to justice. Al and

Sonny along with a number of bodyguards attended a White Sox baseball game. When Sonny relayed this story to me years later, he couldn't remember the stadium where the following event occurred (it was probably Wrigley Field), but what occurred burned an indelible impression in his brain. As he and his father entered on one side of the stadium, President Hoover arrived with his entourage on the opposite side of the stadium. It was the summer of 1931. Hoover was not a popular figure. He was being blamed for the Great Depression and his call for more stringent enforcement of prohibition was equally unpopular to the general populace.

In contrast, Al Capone was providing liquor to anyone who could pay for it and now was feeding thousands of the hungry and unemployed in his soup kitchen. To many people, he was considered a twentieth century Robin Hood.

As Hoover made his appearance, the audience stood but numerous disparaging remarks were heard. As Al Capone entered, the audience turned in his direction and began to cheer wildly. Sonny said, he thought that it was at this moment that Hoover issued orders to "get Capone". Sonny was a young boy, who idolized his father. He had no way of knowing that Internal Revenue Agents at Hoover's direction were already hard at work building a case against his father. The event at the baseball game was probably offensive to the President, but it was hardly the driving motivation.

Al Capone with "Sonny" at Palm Island Estate

Whether or not President Hoover was driven by moral outrage or other political considerations, specifically winning a second term in the White House, the mantra "Get Capone" was on the lips of a small army of federal investigators.

Meanwhile, Mae's fears were growing with every passing week. Instead of admitting even to herself how alarmed she was becoming, she took her cue from Al and if he was nonchalant about the legal issues and just wanted to party, then so would she. She prayed for his safety when she was alone but never stopped smiling and feigning optimism when others were around. Besides, she later said, "there was nothing I could do to stop the dark days from coming, so better to just keep dancing and pray for the strength and courage to face whatever was to come."

chapter thirteen
DAYS OF
HEARTBREAK

Al Capone with his "Sonny" on his First Communion Day 1930

SHORTLY AFTER AL RETURNED FROM Philadelphia in 1930, Mae began to see changes in him. He still loved having the house filled with company, but it was no longer an every night occurrence. He was also putting on weight and slept less and less. He seemed to be constantly going to meetings with attorneys, though he never shared the nature of these meetings with Mae. If she expressed any concerns, he would say to her "don't you worry, dearest, daddy will take care of everything," and so far he had been able to.

Over the course of the rest of 1930 and the early months of 1931, Al was summoned over and over again to hearings with the FBI and IRS. They questioned him repeatedly and ultimately made it clear that they had every intention of trying him for Income Tax evasion. Even so, Al, the consummate optimist, always believed that he would be able to buy his way out of whatever they planned to charge him with. He even attempted to file tax returns for the years in question and was sure that his high priced lawyers would find a way for him to reconcile his situation.

Mae began to finally realize that this time all the prayers in the world weren't going to keep Al safely by her side. All through the hot muggy Chicago summer of 1931 from June 5, when he was formally indicted until July 30, Al's attorneys assured him that they would be able to work out a deal. They told Al that if he were willing to plea bargain, they had been guaranteed that he would not have to go to trial and that his sentence would be less than three years. This was approximately the same sentence that his brother Ralph had received for income tax evasion the year before. If Ralph could do three years in prison (initially Leavenworth and then McNeil Island Penitentiary in Washington), Al figured he could too. He was desperate to get this off his back. He had been looking over his shoulder most of his life, but the Feds were worse than any potential gangland assassin. They didn't have to hide in the bushes or in a dark alley to catch him. They would walk right through his front door and get him and all the bodyguards in the world couldn't stop them.

Al agreed to the plea bargain. In the end, however, Judge James Wilkerson refused to accept the plea agreement and informed Al that he wasn't going to bargain his way out of this situation. He would be going to trial.

The truth of what really transpired in the coming months depends on which version one chooses to believe. We do know that a trial was conducted beginning October 5, 1931. Whether Al tried to buy off jurors; whether Judge Wilkerson's should have recused himself because of personal bias; whether the jury selection was rigged; whether Al's attorneys failed him; whether the pressure from the highest office of the land was the deciding factor and not the case as it was presented, are still questions to this day. What is not in question is the outcome of the trial. Al Capone was convicted of Income Tax evasion and would eventually be sentenced to eleven years in prison. Like everything else that had occurred in his life, Al took the conviction on the chin. There were no histrionics, just the unwavering gaze, the hint of a smile and the handshake with his lawyers and then it was over.

Back at the house on Prairie Avenue, Mae and Sonny waited for the news. Contrary to the reports that Al's family chose not to be at his side, Mae had begged Al to let her be with him in the courtroom. "Even his attorneys thought family presence might evoke some sympathy," Mae pleaded. Al's mind would not be swayed. He had protected her and Sonny all through their lives. He was not about to put her heartbreak on display for the public and he knew that heartbreak was coming even before the verdict was read.

One point worth noting is that at no time during the lead up to the trial, did Al even consider running away. He could have disappeared to any of a number of countries and lived out his life as a wealthy expatriate. "Never", was his response when that was broached. Al saw himself as an American and whatever his fate would be, it would be realized on American soil. One wonders, however, if Al had had any inkling of how long he would be taken from his family and the horror of the place he would finally wind up if he would have so patently rejected the notion of leaving.

Sonny was not nearly so concerned about the outcome as Mae. His father had always taken care of problems and Sonny was confident that Al would sort this business out as well. He didn't realize at the age of thirteen that the precious cocoon he had grown up in would soon be shattered.

As Al left the courthouse, he knew he had to get to Mae and Sonny before anyone else broke the news. Al Capone had faced a lot of hard things in his life including assassin's bullets on many occasions, but nothing had ever been as painful or required more courage than telling Mae and Sonny this awful news. Al held Sonny in his arms when he told him what had happened in court. He smiled and said, "Don't worry, son of my heart, everything will be OK." My attorneys are filing for an appeal of the verdict and it will take some time. You will still see me, but I have to stay at Cook Country jail while the appeals are going on." "You and mom will come often and grandma will bring dinner and it will just be for a few months till we get this worked out. Then we'll go back to Palm Island and I'll never leave you again." "In the meantime, I want you to have a good time at your school and do your best with your studies. I also want you to promise to take care of mom. You will be the man of the house while I'm gone and I need to know that you and mom are O. K." "Can you do that for me, son of my heart, can you do that for your dad?" His father had always taken care of them. In fact he took care of everyone. Sonny smiled through his tears at his father and said, "Don't worry, Dad, I can do it, I won't let you down."

Sonny repeated this story of their goodbye to me many years later when he himself was an old man, and his eyes still filled with tears when he remembered the feeling of fear for the first time in his life at the loss of his father.

In the coming weeks, Sonny and his mother and other members of the family made numerous visits back and forth to Cook County jail. As his father had promised, Grandma Teresa did bring her wonderful Italian feasts and despite the circumstances, Al put on his big smile and poured every ounce of energy, charisma and optimism into convincing his family and most of all Sonny that he was "just grand" and all would be well.

Shortly after Christmas 1931, Mae and Sonny returned to Palm Island without Al. Sonny went immediately back to school and tried as hard as he could to keep his promise to his father. He loved his mother with all his heart and however sad he felt, he would put on a good face for her. Unbeknownst to Sonny, Al had talked with Mae on one of her last visits to see him about the importance of protecting Sonny from the grief and fear they were both feeling. So all three of them repressed their heartbreak and put on a cheerful front to each other and the rest of the world.

The days went by slowly for all three of them. School was a great respite for Sonny. From early in the morning until bedtime, his studies, sports and all his new friends kept him occupied. He was enrolled at St. Patrick's Catholic School in Miami Beach, Florida. For the first time in his life there were lots of boys and girls his own age to play sports with and talk to. He knew there were times when some kids were forbidden to come to his home on Palm Island, but there were lots of others who were warm and friendly and many of them became lifelong friends.

At night, however, Sonny was alone with his thoughts of his father and sometimes the fear he might never see him again. After his mother would come in to say his prayers with him and say goodnight, he could finally allow the tears to come. Sometimes he found he had to press his mouth against his pillow to stifle his sobs, just as his mother, Mae, was doing in her lavish, but lonely room down the hall.

Sonny felt as if his whole world had fallen apart. His beloved father had been taken away from him and from Sonny's perspective it would be an eternity before he would come home. He knew his mother felt the same way. She tried not to show her tears, but her eyes were always red and her delightful laugh seemed permanently silenced. The days became weeks and still there was no word of encouragement from Al's lawyers. Every couple of weeks, Mae would board the train for the trip to Chicago leaving Sonny at school and under the watchful eye of Muriel and Louie.

For the next several months, Al was housed at the Cook County Jail on a contempt of court sentence. At least there, he was able to see his family frequently; have his own meals brought in (often by his mother); continue running his business and even have intimate times with Mae in a most accommodating warden's office. In May, the words they were dreading finally came: "appeals denied." All attempts at appeal had been exhausted. After serving seven months in Cook County, Al was to be moved by train immediately to the Federal Penitentiary in Atlanta to serve out the balance of his eleven year sentence. Al reacted to this news as he had that gray day in October when he was first sentenced, "he took the blow and let it go." He was a man and he would deal with whatever he had to, but the thought of what this would do to Mae and Sonny was a knife though his heart.

Again, Al realized he had to break it to them himself before the news media got wind of it. The thought of breaking their hearts as he knew this news would was the most painful thing he had ever faced. He feared, too, that it might destroy the thing he valued most in life, the love and adoration of the two people he loved most on earth. With a heavy heart and tears in his eyes, he sent for his loved ones.

In May of 1932, the Dixie Flyer departed the train station in Chicago heading south to the Federal Penitentiary in Atlanta. At many train stops, curious onlookers waved at Al like he was a celebrity and Al smiled and waved back. He was a man and he would take this like a man. He never showed fear or even anxiety. His amazing capacity for optimism regardless of the circumstances had never failed him, at least not yet. He would do what he had to do, just as he had all his life. There would be no self-pity, no sign of fear or weakness. He told reporters traveling on the Dixie Flyer to Atlanta with him on May 4, 1932, "I'll take what they give me for two reasons - one is the only way you can expect to get a pardon is to go along and be a good prisoner and the other is, I won't have any say about it." Al was nothing if not a pragmatist.

Al Capone on his way to Federal Penitentiary in Atlanta May, 1932

Numerous accounts of Al's time in Atlanta indicate that he was a cooperative and congenial inmate. In fact some called him a "model prisoner". His cellmate recounted that his favorite topic of conversation was his beautiful wife and his beloved son. The only time he became agitated was when the warden suddenly changed prison policy limiting family visits. Al promptly wrote a most courteous letter of appeal to the warden to allow some flexibility for family visitors who had to travel a great distance as all of his family did. Apparently, that was the only time that the warden made any concessions and it was not just for Al's visitation privileges. Other prisoners and their families were also affected. Even though he was taunted by some prisoners, who perceived that he was buying extra privileges, he tried to avoid being baited. Al was determined to keep his head down and do his time as stoically as possible.

Over the coming years, he did just what he said, Al toughed it out. Despite rumors from some that Al was given preferential treatment, Warden A. C. Aderhold flatly denied them. The warden further said that because there was concern that Al might try to escape or continue running his business enterprise from behind bars, rules for his visitors were more stringently applied than for anyone else. In his reports he further indicated that he found Prisoner 40886, Al Capone, cooperative and cheerful. Mae, Sonny and the other members of Al's family visited him regularly throughout his time there. At every opportunity, Al assured Mae he would never do anything that might jeopardize his time off for good behavior. All he cared about, he told her, was to come home to Sonny and her as soon as possible.

Unfortunately, given the publicity of his life and exploits, not to mention the public's insatiable fascination with news of Al Capone, it was almost impossible for him to keep a low profile. Other prisoners often either courted his favor in hopes of access to his wealth, or the more envious hatefully did anything to provoke a reaction that would send him to solitary. Some prisoners even sold stories about Al to the media. The more outrageous the stories, the more money they were worth. The truth of his days of tedium, humiliation and sadness wouldn't sell nearly as well as scandalous reports that he was buying favors and getting special treatment.

Regardless of how long he had been in prison, that man's name could still sell newspapers and to many newsmen the more colorful and sensational the stories of Al Capone's time in prison the better. Truth was irrelevant.

Despite rumors of Al "doing easy time" and even being permitted to leave the prison for family visitations, nothing could be further from the truth. If anything, prison rules were more stringent for him. No guard and certainly no warden wanted to be accused of being paid to go easy on Public Enemy No. 1.

These stories did have an impact on Al and his future even though they were false. Those in charge of law enforcement would not be made to appear bungling or inept again. Al had made fools of the law and those who enforce it long enough. For years his empire had thrived because of the complicity and corruption in the Chicago police department and the state and federal courts. Federal law enforcement was in charge now and they would demonstrate their power once and for all. They would make an example of Al Capone. Never again would anyone claim that he was doing "easy time".

Two years and three months after arriving at Atlanta, Al was shocked to learn that he was being transferred to the most forbidding high-security prison in the country: Alcatraz. In August of 1934, with no advance notification and apparently no justification other than to make an example of him to other criminals, Al was shackled and placed on a train for the trip from Atlanta to what was called "the Rock". Nothing Al had ever experienced in his life could have prepared him for the torment of the next four and a half years.

Despite Mae's devastation at the news, like Al, she was a pragmatist. One way or another, they would survive. When it was over, she and Sonny would be waiting with open arms for Al, and the three of them would never again be parted. Had she known anything about "the Rock" she might not have been so confident. Throughout these awful, lonely years Mae's faith along with her unwavering love for Sonny and Al were all that sustained her.

chapter fourteen
THE TRIP TO HELL
1934

THE FOLLOWING STORY IS ONE my grandmother told me in 1976. It is unforgettable. This is the story Al told her in 1940 when he was finally home from what he called "his hell". He said that the nightmare had begun shortly after dinner on August 18, 1934, while he was incarcerated in the Atlanta Penitentiary. Al was showing Red "Rusty" Rudensky, his cellmate, the new picture of Sonny that he had just received in his latest letter from Mae.

"Sonny" Capone, photo sent to Al while in prison in Atlanta

Suddenly two guards appeared at the entrance to his cell and said, "Come on, Al, the warden wants to see you." Al had been in Atlanta for over two years by this time. He had had ups and downs over the years and had been summoned by the warden before. It had never been a big deal. Warden Aderhold sent for him once in a while and sometimes Al even requested a meeting with him. Aderhold found Al very cooperative and so far they had never had a serious problem. Somehow, he intuitively sensed this time was different. "What's up?" he asked the guard as three other guards joined the first two. Rusty, his cellmate and confidant looked up with alarm. Something about this seemed ominous to him as well. Al started backing away holding Sonny's photograph in his hands. "Just leave your stuff here and come with us, we don't want any trouble."

Al hadn't managed to stay alive over the years without pretty good instincts and just as he began to sense he was in eminent danger, he heard an inmate snarl from a nearby cell, "The big guy is going to the Rock." Al tried to fight off the guards and swore they would never take him away. Several more guards entered the fray and when Rusty tried to intercede for his friend, he was knocked unconscious. Al fought like a madman and howled obscenities until he too, was knocked unconscious. It took seven guards to remove him from the cell. Rusty never saw Al again.

It was a little after midnight, on August 19, when Al, along with 52 other prisoners, was loaded onto two armored train cars. With leg irons and their wrists manacled, the prisoners were then shackled to each other two by two. There were bars on the windows and steel mesh screening which prevented anyone seeing in or out. The two prison cars were heavily guarded. Attached to the prison cars were four other cars to accommodate the guards, the train crew and the warden. Warden Aderhold accompanied the prisoners on this three-day voyage across the country from Atlanta to northern California making sure that nothing would go wrong. Every precaution had been taken and great secrecy was observed to prevent any attempt at escape or hijacking of prisoners.

Al told Mae years later that his greatest fear throughout these years of imprisonment was that he would be murdered either by another inmate or the guards. Now on this god awful train as temperatures outside reached well over a hundred degrees, he began to think the greatest risk was sweltering to death. He said throughout the nightmare journey when he felt that he couldn't take much more, the thought of being with her and his beloved Sonny again was all that kept him going.

By the end of the three-day ordeal, Al had lost all sense of time and reality. He repeated the prayer, "please dear God, don't let me die," so many times that later the prayer and the heat were all he could remember. Finally, he realized that the jarring motion of the train had stopped. Someone was pulling on him to stand up and it took all the strength and power his 35 year old tortured legs had to drag himself up on his feet. When he did, he realized that the iron shackles that had been cutting into his flesh had been removed. He moved forward with the rest of the men toward the door of the train car and for the first time in days inhaled a breath of fresh air, salty moist cool fresh air.

The men were ordered to climb up the steep rocky hill to a large cement structure at the top of the Island of Pelicans (Alcatraz). It felt good to move, but the relief of being able to move their cramped bodies and finally breathe clean air was short lived. The reality of what was awaiting them filled Al with a sick dread akin to the horror of knowing one is to be buried alive, he would tell Mae years later. Al Capone had reached the end of his journey. He wondered, rightly so, if he would ever survive what was to come. In many ways the man he was when he entered that awful place on August 22nd did not survive. But perhaps the broken, seriously ill man who left Alcatraz many years later was more impressive than the one who had entered it on that foggy summer day. This place robbed him of everything: his freedom, his dignity, his riches and power, not to mention what he loved most in life, his family. It also took away his arrogance, his ruthlessness, his greed, his capacity for violence and his twisted ability to rationalize the atrocities he had committed. It even took away his name. While he was in Alcatraz, he was never given the pride and privilege of hearing his own name. Al Capone became number 85 and that was all. He was no longer famous. There were no longer news photographers jockeying to take his picture. No more young women hoping to catch his eye. No more feelings of importance and dominance. He wasn't a big shot anymore.

.... And yet, it gave him back something more priceless than all the riches and power in the world. In the darkness and despair of Alcatraz, Al Capone said that he believed that he had been given a second chance at life.

Al got through the horror and loneliness of his days in Alcatraz like a man lost in a nightmare that just went on and on. He said that the monotony of the days was broken only by moments of sheer terror. The fear of being murdered was his constant companion. Over and over he whispered the prayer, "please dear God, don't let me die," just as he had on the trip across country. Even that grueling trip had almost faded from his memory. He often had trouble remembering that there had ever been anything else but the darkness and cold of this place. From the day he had become prisoner number 85, every waking moment was dictated by Warden Johnston and the guards. For the most part, all prisoners were kept in silence. Once they were allowed to have yard privileges, they were able to speak for a few minutes each day, but he was constantly being warned to "be quiet" in the dining room and moving through the rest of his day.

Prisoners were rousted early at Alcatraz. They were taken from their cells by 6:30, a. m. , and after breakfast were sent to their respective jobs: the laundry, the kitchen, the cobbler shop, one cleaning crew or another and if one was lucky, the library. In mid-day they were given lunch and then sent back to their work until late afternoon. Taken next to their cells and called out to be counted, they then filed down to the dining room and after eating in silence again were sent back to their cells, day after day, week after week. Shortly after Al arrived he was assigned to the laundry where prisoners washed their clothes and bedding and that of the staff on the island. Often they were required to also do laundry for nearby military facilities.

It was mind numbing work. The only thing a prisoner did have to remain alert to was the danger of his hands being mangled if he did not move them quickly enough. In Al's case, he also had to stay alert to the threat of attack by other inmates. This was something he lived with every moment of his time at Alcatraz. Despite the rule of silence, word got around readily enough surreptitiously. Al had been repeatedly approached for money to facilitate one hare brained escape plot or another. Often other prisoners would attempt to extort money from him for protection. When he refused, which he always did, he became the target of their frustration and aggression. Some prisoners even falsely accused him of masterminding escape plots or any other transgression they could think of that might cost him time in solitary. So far, it had been to no avail.

Then in February, 1935, Al was working in the laundry feeding clothing through a mangle. The inmate working with him, Bill Collier, who hated Al and had been spoiling for a chance to get at him, found an opportunity. He complained that Al was deliberately pushing the sopping laundry through the machine too fast. Al ignored him and continued. Collier grabbed a large bundle of wet laundry and heaved it at Al's head. Al turned and slugged the man in the face and a brawl ensued. Guards hauled both men to the "hole" (solitary confinement) and they were kept in there for the next eight days. There was nothing but darkness, a damp cold darkness that not a speck of light or the slightest sound could penetrate. It was an aloneness and a darkness that one hears about in horror stories and this felt like a horror story.

Al had been very careful while he was living through his time in prison never to hint to Mae the fears and threats he dealt with every day of the over eight years. These stories were not talked about at all until years later when he was home safely in her arms. But, when he finally did talk about it, the horror poured out of him, and the worst of it was the solitary confinement. Once he told her these stories, he would never speak of them again.

Al said that first day in solitary, in what felt like night, he was put in a place that was more like death than he had ever imagined. It all seemed to have happened so suddenly. The scuffle with Collier had been brewing for a long time, but when it finally erupted, it was like an explosion. Al had tried hard to avoid being baited into any kind of situation that might cause him to lose his time off for good behavior. He had promised Mae he would keep his head down, no matter what happened. All that mattered was getting through this and getting home to her and Sonny. Now he had let himself react. He had let himself fight back and look where it got him. He didn't know how long he would be kept in this darkness and as moments ticked by, or days, he had no sense of time at all. It was like eternity.

Initially, he pounded his head with his fists. "How could you let that weasel get to you, you fool?" He was actually madder at himself than Collier. Now he was here in this darkness. The cell walls were made of thick concrete as was the floor. There was nothing in the darkness but the walls and the floor and some kind of drain or container that smelled like human waste. He sat on the floor for an inestimable period of time in silence. His thoughts and his breath were his only companions. At some point, two slices of bread and a tin cup of water were shoved through a small slot at the bottom of the door to the cell. Al called out to the guards, but they said nothing.

Inmates at Alcatraz talked with dread about the "hole". Many of them had experienced it. They all agreed that it would drive a man mad. Even a few days in solitary took a toll on a person's sanity. They agreed that more than a couple of weeks there was enough to drive anybody permanently "off his rocker." There is no clock in solitary that allows one to monitor the passing of time. There is no way to know if it is day or night. A prisoner was never informed of how long he must stay in this cold forbidding darkness.

Al told Mae later that he prayed while he was in solitary, he cried out in frustration and he prayed. At first, his prayers were only that he would survive, that he would get to see her and Sonny again. As the hours in the cold and the darkness ebbed by, he thought about his life and all that had brought him to this place. There was never a point even in his desperation that he wished to die. At some point in that darkness, Al later described to Mae, what he thought was a dream. He told her that he had no idea how long he had been in solitary when this profound and surreal experience occurred, but there was no question that it had occurred and he could, even years later, recall it vividly.

Al described the experience to her in the only way that it made sense to him. He said he believed that in the midst of his anguish, he had cried out to God for mercy and forgiveness and somehow felt a light had been turned on in his head. He said his whole life seemed laid out like a tapestry in front of him. He felt that he could stand back like a blind man who had just been given the gift of sight and scrutinize the whole dazzling horrific spectacle. He thought for a minute maybe this is the flash of my whole life before my eyes in the seconds before I die that people talk about. He said he didn't feel afraid; in fact he felt somehow comforted. He knew he had made mistakes and had done some terrible things which he would probably be judged harshly for, but he felt nothing but a kind of warmth and peace. He said, "it was a peace I have never felt before". At some point time passed and he had the sense that he was waking from a wonderful dream. For the first time since he arrived at Alcatraz, in fact for the first time since he had been taken away to prison, he knew he would survive. He knew he was being given another chance and no matter what he had to go through, he would survive and return to his family. Somehow he would find a way to make amends.

Many biographers later wrote about Al's sudden embrace of religion implying that it was a byproduct of his mental impairment which occurred during his incarceration. Even some of the most scholarly biographers have insinuated that syphilis which caused his mental decline in the later part of his life is what set the stage for a real or perhaps imagined spiritual conversion. This is unfortunate because it undermines and diminishes the almost miraculous and certainly profound transformation that occurred while he was in Alcatraz.

chapter fifteen
SON OF MY HEART

MEANWHILE IN FLORIDA, MAE AND Sonny were unaware of what was happening to Al. Mae had been totally distraught in August of 1934 to learn that Al had been moved to Alcatraz. She had never heard of Alcatraz before Al was taken there, and now that she had learned what this awful place was like she longed for the days of ignorance. Months had gone by since she had last seen Al. Not for one night was she able to relinquish her sense of dread that Al might never survive the loneliness and desperation of Alcatraz's horrors. Until Al was home, she would remain a prisoner just like him. The only thing that briefly assuaged her days and nights of torment were Al's letters. Al Capone was not a learned man, but his letters to Mae and Sonny were pure poetry and filled with hope. Al was always cheerful, loving and encouraging in those letters home.

Al was only allowed to write one letter each week and they were always sent to Mae and Sonny. Mae was never able to see his handwriting without tears welling up in her eyes. Those letters addressed to her always began with "dearest" and those to Sonny were addressed to "son of my heart".

Never one time did Al reveal in his letters to Mae and Sonny what his days and nights were really like. He spoke only of what he was reading (he was now working in the prison library) or films he had seen. Often he described meals he had eaten and always he spoke of the joy they would share when he returned to them. As time went by he began to speak of the young Catholic seminarian who came to talk with him every week. He also told Mae he had gone to Confession and was now regularly receiving communion. Eventually, Al spoke of learning to read music, play musical instruments and of the songs that he was writing for her.

She sent pictures of herself and Sonny to him frequently and always made sure they had big smiles on their faces She knew how much seeing their faces meant to him and knowing that they were both well and happy.

Three photos of Mae and Sonny at Palm Island sent to Alcatraz (always with big smiles to reassure Al)

Mae's life revolved around those letters from Al and seeing to Sonny's care.

Mae was determined that Sonny would have as happy a life as was possible. She encouraged him to bring his friends home and was a gracious hostess to all those who attended the frequent parties on the Island during Sonny's years at St. Patrick's School. As always, her faith continued to sustain her. She read with profound gladness especially those letters in which Al spoke of praying and reaching out to God. Mae had always believed that God's grace was the only real solace in their "veil of tears".

After Al was first taken to Alcatraz, months went by before Mae was allowed to see him. When she was, it took days of train travel to cross the country and then to ride the ferry boat out to the forbidding windswept island in the San Francisco Bay. Each time she would make that grueling trip, she was required to first write the warden for permission to visit. She complied with every requirement. She would do anything to see Al's face for the few minutes that she was allowed. She and Al both agreed that she would not bring Sonny on these visits. Sonny never went to Alcatraz until shortly before the end of Al's time there.

Thanks to their letters, the intensity of their bond of affection never wavered; in fact it grew during those long years of separation. The letters from Mae and Sonny were equally sustaining to Al. He loved hearing about Sonny's sporting and school events and about his friends. It thrilled him to think his son was having as happy and normal a life as possible under the circumstances. Of particular interest to Al was the mention Sonny now made regularly of a new girlfriend at school. He seemed quite taken with this red haired Irish girl, whom he called "Casey". It made Al smile to think that like himself, his son was drawn to an Irish girl. He could hardly wait to hear more about her.

chapter sixteen
CASEY

Diana Ruth Casey age 16

DIANA RUTH CASEY FIRST SAW Albert Francis "Sonny" Capone in September of 1934. They were both enrolled at St. Patrick's Catholic School in Miami Beach, Florida. Diana Ruth Casey (later to be called "Casey" by Sonny and then all her friends) was a tall slender auburn haired young girl, who had just moved to Florida from her ancestral home in Chattanooga, Tennessee. For years, her well to do family had wintered in Florida, but her parents had finally had enough of the Tennessee weather and decided to move the whole family including their young son and maternal grandmother to the land of sunshine permanently.

Casey had just begun her freshman year at St. Patrick's Catholic School and was already smitten with the classic Spanish architecture of the buildings, the lush tropical gardens and most of all, her teachers, the brilliant and inspirational Dominican nuns. They were the epitome of every virtue she admired.

Casey was a devoutly Catholic young girl, a conscientious student and an avid writer, even at the age of fourteen. As an only child for much of her early years, who was not close during those years to her often traveling and partying parents, Casey had always found solace in her faith, her writing and her books.

The move to Florida had been a good one for her. The birth of her little brother and only sibling a few years before and now this new life in Florida brought cohesion to the family she felt had been missing before.

Her journal, which had often been filled with feelings of isolation and loneliness, now reflected youthful enthusiasm and optimism. In one of the entries during her first year in Miami Beach, she recounted first seeing Sonny:

> September 1934: "my first glimpse of this shy, appealing boy was in St. Patrick's Church where Confession was a Saturday afternoon ritual. As he walked down the aisle, shirt-tail loose from recent activity on the handball court, his hair brushing his forehead, I thought, he's cute; I hope I get to meet him some day."

Only a few days later, "I saw him again", she wrote; this time being picked up from the high school by a driver in a dark Cadillac sedan. Sonny caught her eye, smiled and waved as he rode away. She turned to her new friend, Peggy Brennan, and asked, "Wow, who is that?" "He is Sonny Capone, Al Capone's son."

Casey came from a very sheltered background, but even she knew that name. "He goes to school here?" "Yeah, he is a really nice guy. He is a year ahead of us." Peggy said.

A few days later, several young people were standing in front of the high school. As Casey walked out of the main entrance with Peggy, her eyes again met those of Sonny Capone. There was an instant electrifying connection between them. Another young student named Jack Harkness, who was a recent acquaintance of hers, was standing next to Sonny. As the girls approached, Jack looked up and said to her, " I'd like to introduce you to Sonny Capone." Jack said the attraction between them was unmistakable, but no one had any idea how much this meeting would change their lives. In years to come both Jack Harkness and Peggy Brennan would be in Casey and Sonny's wedding party.

Casey wrote in her journal entry dated, <u>September 28, 1934</u>:

> *"I met the nicest boy at school today. He was likable, friendly and attractive, with thick dark hair and brows above expressive blue green eyes. Hope I get to see him again."*

In the coming school year, Casey frequently saw Sonny at school, church and at parties with other St. Pat's kids.

> <u>*May, 1935*</u>*: "Sonny loved to entertain at his home on the Island, where those student-classmates who were 'allowed to attend the Capone home' enjoyed the gala swim-buffet parties at the estate. His mother was always present along with other adults to chaperone, at least in the background."*

'I am very glad to know you, Mrs. Capone, I remember saying to her the first time we met, to which she answered formally, 'likewise, dear.... '

Her son's friends who were regular visitors called Mrs. Capone 'Aunt Mae'. This seemed comfortable to me, after a while. It is funny how habits start. In the same way, when Al and I later met, he would become 'Uncle Al'."

One of Casey's more amusing journal entries was about an incident that occurred once when Sonny was walking her home from school carrying her books.

> <u>*April, 1936*</u>*: "My family home is on Prairie Avenue in Miami Beach. It is less than two miles from school*

and I often walk home with a friend. Whenever I walk home with Sonny, a driver follows in a dark sedan. On this particular afternoon, we got into an argument about something stupid and he threw my books on the sidewalk. For the first time in my life, but not the last, my red-headed Irish temper got the best of me. I stalked off to my home leaving the books where they lay. Sonny, equally piqued, was not about to pick the books up and follow me home. So he called the driver to come and get my books and take them to my house. He was not going to leave my books on the ground, but he also had no intention of showing up at our front door carrying them."

Whatever the source of their friction, it didn't last long. They became close friends, in fact, sweethearts, and were quite inseparable throughout high school.

<u>May, 1936:</u> *"Our first real date was the Junior-Senior High School Prom. It was a double-date and Sonny brought me a white orchid wrist corsage. We danced to the music of the Tommy Dorsey band, and boy, could he dance! I love Sonny Capone."*

chapter seventeen
FINDING HIS WAY BACK

"Though I walk through the valley of the shadow of death"
(Psalm 23:4)

AL CAPONE SPENT 1,597 DAYS or four years and five months in prison on Alcatraz. This penal institution which was called an experiment in government sadism by some, and a hell hole by others became the means by which Al found his way back to his humanity. Surrounded by many prisoners who swore to get Capone for no other reason than to put their forgettable names in the history books for being the one who killed him, Al fought every day for survival in this place. There were reports of a number of physical attacks including stabbings as well as murderous plots including someone putting lye into his coffee. These were played down by the Warden Johnston, who believed he had everything under control.

Some of the incidents did become public and Al's family lived in terror that one of these attempts would be successful. Mae and Al's family wrote numerous letters to the Warden pleading for Al's transfer to another prison, but to no avail. The fear Al lived with was something he never mentioned until long after when he was finally home.

Al had always tried to reassure his family that he was all right. His letters sounded quite upbeat when he talked about books he had read or the music he had taught himself to play. Then Mae began to see a glimmer of other even more encouraging changes in Al's letters, despite the effort of the prison censors to obfuscate all but the most mundane and superficial messages. Mae realized that the prayers for her and Sonny that Al often mentioned perfunctorily had become a more significant theme in his letters. He sounded more at peace than he had in all the years he had been away. Even in "the shadows of the valley of death, I will fear no evil if Thou art with me", it says in the Bible. His letters sounded like he had found that truth for the first time in his adult life.

The prison censors were ruthless in deleting many whole sentences in the one letter Al was allowed to write each week to his wife or family. It seemed that the last thing these censors wanted was for the word to get out to the public that Al Capone had been sent to a living hell and found God.

For years, while living on Prairie Avenue in Chicago, Mae and Al's mother, Teresa, had attended daily mass, always praying for Al's safety. They also prayed for his soul. It had become apparent to Mae, though she never let on to anyone, that Al had crossed into a world of darkness during those years, where any act of violence could be justified as "part of business". For a deeply devout Catholic woman, it was her dream that someday Al would embrace the faith that he, too, had been born into and become the good man she believed he could be.

It was not uncommon for men of their generation, including those who were raised in the Catholic tradition, to leave the praying to the women. Now over and over again in his letters, Al referred to the wonderful talks he was having with a young Jesuit seminarian, who came weekly to Alcatraz. Between the devastating despair he had felt in solitary confinement, which

Mae perceived seemed to have brought about a profound change; the encouragement of the Jesuit seminarian, Michael Casey; and the new-found hope he began to express in his letters, Mae began to feel that Al was really on his way back to becoming the person she married. She continued to pray for that.

Then in February 1938, word leaked out to the newspaper, that Al Capone had experienced some kind of breakdown. Mae knew that he had been diagnosed with syphilis many years before. She also knew that he had undergone potent treatments while incarcerated to reduce the progression of the disease. Was this a reaction to the disease? Was it a reaction to the treatments? Was it possibly something more sinister, like another attempted poisoning which had brought on a breakdown? Mae and the family were desperate for information about Al's condition. She sent a telegram to Warden Johnston immediately and waited days to learn from the warden that Al was comfortable and stable in the prison hospital.

"Sonny" age 19 on the diving board at Palm Island

Mae pleaded to be allowed to see Al and was told to wait. It was not until seven months later and after numerous letters requesting visitation that Mae was finally permitted to see her husband. It would be one of the last times she would have to make that dreaded journey by ferry boat to the forbidding monolith, Alcatraz Island. This time she would be accompanied by Sonny.

Mae gripped the rail of the ferry boat as the damp breeze of the foggy San Francisco Bay chilled her to the bone. While Al's letters had been reassuring of late, she had no clear idea how she would find him. Her heart was filled with equal parts trepidation and anticipation at the thought of finally seeing him.

It seemed impossible to believe she had survived these years without Al. She doubted she would have without her beloved son and family and of course her faith. She wondered just then as she looked at Sonny, what was going through his mind. Was he fearful of the changes he would see in his father? Had the years and time apart taken a toll on the adoration he had felt for his father when he was a little boy? Would he be brave when the visit ended? At the age of 19, Sonny had become a man. Mae felt great pride in this son she had raised. He had been privileged materially and was gifted with a good mind and a kind heart, but what losses he also had to endure. Despite whatever he had been through, Sonny was a happy person. He was never bitter or cynical. At last, after all these years, he would see his father again and Mae hoped he would be as strong as she tried to be when she visited Al.

Al, too, was anxious. He had just received the latest picture of Sonny taken at the pool on Palm Island. For the first time Al realized his son had become a man. He was no longer the little boy who idolized his father. Al wondered if this beautiful young man would still feel the same about him after all these years.

Finally, the ferry boat carrying Mae and Sonny pulled up to the dock and they were there. At last, she would see the face she had so longed to touch. At last, there would be that brave smile filled with warmth and optimism that broke her heart. Al always tried to allay her fears and put on a cheerful expression. Now in just a few minutes they would see him.

Mae and Sonny waited patiently on the visitors' side of the steel door. Then she heard the sound of the window cover being moved aside. Sonny leaned forward pressing his face against the door. Al blinked several times in disbelief when the beautiful blue green eyes, so much like his own, appeared at the small window. The little square window in the massive steel door was only slightly larger than an index card. Al gasped at the sight of those eyes he knew so well. He whispered the words, "son of my heart", the phrase he often addressed Sonny with in his letters and in the long conversations he had with him in his head during so many sleepless nights. Al asked his son to stand back so he could see the full length of him. He let his breath out slowly, awed by the sight he had dreamed of for so long, Sonny and Mae, the loves of his life. The three of them were together. Even this horrible place and the barricade between them couldn't diminish the joy of being in each other's company at last. There were tears, but they were tears of joy. Al knew now that he would survive, and survive he did.

He spent the rest of his time at Alcatraz in the prison hospital. His behavior fluctuated between being erratic and then docile and compliant. He clearly was not the same man who had entered Alcatraz, not mentally, not physically and not spiritually. He believed the doctors treated him well at the hospital and later Al actually praised the care he had been given there, even though his doctors in years to come said that his care had been quite deficient. Finally, on January 5, 1939, Al left that hell on earth. The Al Capone he had been when he arrived in August of 1934 had died on that desolate island. The man he had become was taken by boat and then by train to Terminal Island in Southern California where he would serve the final months of his sentence.

Physically, Al still seemed massive, but after years in Alcatraz, he was 40 to 50 pounds lighter than when he had arrived. Gone was the thick dark hair he had as a young man, the top of his head was balding. Gone, too, were the swagger in his walk and the sneer that had often frightened his enemies. These physical changes didn't begin to match the changes that had occurred inside his heart. He was well aware that his mind was not always his own or at least not something he could count on as before. There were times when he blacked out entirely, and when he finally felt that he was himself again, wasn't sure how much time had elapsed. It didn't happen every day, but when it did occur, he had no idea what had come over him. It felt as if he had gone into an altered state that he could never quite recall. Al knew he had changed both mentally and physically, but these changes seemed insignificant compared to the sense of serenity of which he was now also aware. After years of living with the double-edged sword of violence and fear, he knew a degree of peace he had never experienced in his previous life. There were times when the "old Al" would surface and couldn't quite reconcile this new perspective. He wondered "where his old companions fear and violence had gone?" Later when he was home on the Island, he would describe this to Mae, but he never tried to share it with his brothers. He knew they would never understand. Mae would understand though, as she understood everything about him.

During the ten months Al spent at Terminal Island, Sonny and Mae came again for short visits and finally they came for the last time and when they left, he left with them. Mae and Ralph, after numerous discussions with medical experts, had decided that it was best for Al to try a new treatment for syphilis. Al concurred. Now that he was free to return to Palm Island with his loved ones, he wanted all the time he could get.

Al's next stop before his return to Palm Island was thus to Johns Hopkins Hospital in Baltimore, Maryland. He was ultimately moved to Union Memorial Hospital nearby. There he was placed under the care of Dr. Joseph E. Moore, a specialist renowned for treatment of venereal disease. Dr. Moore told Mae after a thorough examination of Al and a review of his records, that the care he had received in prison was "inadequate". Al then willingly endured months of torturous treatments under Dr. Moore's expert direction in hopes of staving off the final stages of his now incurable disease.

It was March of 1940 when Al returned to his beloved island sanctuary. The island hadn't changed much over the years. If anything, it was even more beautiful than he remembered. The warm tropical breezes and the constant affection of Mae and Sonny were the best medicine in the world. Within weeks of his return, his mother and sister and all his brothers made trips to Florida to see him. Other friends and relatives were asked to wait before visiting so he could regain his strength after the rigorous treatments he had gone through. Al wanted to see everyone, but Mae was now the boss and taking care of Al was all that mattered to her. She would not allow anyone near him who would cause him stress or agitation. Anyone who wanted to come to the island had to get Mae's approval.

It wasn't long before Al began to feel healthier and happier than he had in a long time, maybe ever. The gift that had come with his disease was that he was no longer considered a threat to his old enemies or a rival to his allies. Syphilis had become his ticket out of "the business". "That's right," he told Mae, "syphilis was a gift."

Once Al felt well settled at home, his first request was to meet Sonny's girl, "Casey". Al couldn't wait to meet her. Al knew something that Mae didn't. This was the girl Sonny wanted to marry.

chapter eighteen
DAYS OF JOY AND GRATITUDE

FROM THE FIRST DAY SHE met Al Capone, Casey was charmed by him as the following entries will attest. These excerpts were selected from her private journals written between 1937 and 1941. I did not know about the journals my mother kept until long after her death in 1989.

September 1937: "*Sonny and I have been dating throughout high school. Sonny enrolled in the University of Notre Dame in South Bend, Indiana last month to begin working on his Bachelor's degree. We spent so many wonderful days together throughout the summer and now sadly I don't know when I will see him, probably not until Christmas.*"

October 1937: "*I just got a call from Sonny and he wants me to fly up for the Homecoming football game this weekend. Mother said I could go and I am so excited. The campus of Notre Dame is so beautiful and I know I will love it and the cool autumn weather. All the trees have turned red and gold and it is so different from Miami Beach. Sonny was really glad to see me as I was to see him. What a thrill to wear the blue and gold chrysanthemum corsage Sonny bought me and cheer on "The Fighting Irish" football team. I loved being there with him and his college friends.*"

Christmas 1937: "Oh, it is so wonderful having Sonny home for Christmas and I got a great surprise. His mother has asked him to transfer from Notre Dame to the University of Miami after he finishes his freshmen year, so when he comes home this summer he won't be going back up north. His mom said she wants him home when his dad comes back, but I think it is just that she is really missing him, and Sonny will do anything she asks."

January 1938: "I am thrilled that Sonny will be back in Florida and especially at the University where I will be enrolling next fall. I understand how much it means to him and to his mother to be nearby when Sonny's dad returns home. The sadness of having his father away has been something that Sonny had been living with for years even before I met him. Finally, that sadness will go away. I don't know when his father will return, but it seems it must be fairly soon."

January 1940: "After months and months of waiting, Sonny finally told me that his father, Al, will be home on Palm Island within weeks. Al is undergoing some medical treatments and is currently hospitalized in Baltimore. For the first couple of months after his return, few guests other than family will be invited to the house. Al will be recuperating and needs his rest, all were told."

April 1940: "At last the day has come. Sonny said his father wants to meet me. I later learned that Al wanted to meet me from the first week he returned to Florida, but Sonny's mother (whom I now called Aunt Mae as do all Sonny's other friends) wanted to wait. On that warm April afternoon when Sonny brought me to the Island, I was filled with excitement. I thought of Al as the beloved father of my fiancé (though our engagement is still being kept a secret), not as someone of notoriety. As Al approached Sonny and me, I saw him only as a pleasant, smiling man in a white suit coming to welcome me. He extended his hand to me, a gesture which ended in his bending for-

"Sonny" and "Casey" in 1940
Palm Island

ward to kiss my hand. I felt very much at ease with him. Al Capone is now forty one years of age and of large stature. Though already balding, he retains a thick fringe of curly dark hair, becoming to his full face. He appeared to be just a shade under six feet tall. Heavy dark brows and lashes framed his strikingly beautiful blue gray eyes. Later when he turned away from me, I caught a glimpse of a narrow scar on the side of his face, not especially evident except in a side view. In any case, it was subordinate to the good natured countenance of the man."

<u>May 1940</u>: *"What a lovely man Uncle Al is. I have been in his company a number of times by now and he insists on being called "Uncle Al". Mr. Capone was just too formal, he said, especially since I call Sonny's mother, Aunt Mae. Uncle Al was the quintessential host. He loved having the house full of family and friends. He loved music, he loved laughter, he loved life, but mostly he adored Mae and Sonny. Anyone who was a friend of Sonny's was welcomed with open arms. I was treated to the warmth of Al's affection from the first meeting as was my little brother, Jim, who often comes to the Capone home with me."*

<u>July 1940</u>: *"My little brother, Jim, just dotes on Uncle Al. It is hard to go to Sonny's house without him tagging along. I sometimes pay him a quarter to stay in his room when Sonny comes to pick me up. I love my brother, but I don't really want to take him on dates with us. If he finds out I'm going to Sonny's house, he just hangs around the front door*

waiting till Sonny comes knowing that he'll be invited to join us. Then when we get there, he acts like Uncle Al is his playmate. He loves playing in the pool with him and Uncle Al seems to enjoy it just as much. There the two of them are laughing and splashing around in the pool and my brother is up on Uncle Al's shoulders as if they are his private diving platform. All the while Uncle Al is encouraging him to work on his dives."

"Casey" and brother Jim 1939

August 1940: *"I have come to understand the depth of Sonny's affection for his dad. Uncle Al is the kindest and most loving father I have ever been around. I love my dad too, but I have never had the closeness to him that Sonny has with his father. I have also grown to understand that Uncle Al is my ally. He always complements me especially when Aunt Mae is around. Every once in a while he*

Al Capone enjoying a swim at Palm Island 1940

winks at me conspiratorially. I am beginning to think that Sonny might have told him about our secret engagement. Sonny doesn't want to say anything to his mom about our plans till after he graduates next June. He says his mom has been through such a hard time with his father away. He just wants to give her some time to enjoy being a family again. Sonny dotes on his mom and will do anything to make her happy."

chapter nineteen

PEACE AT LAST ON PALM ISLAND

AL CAPONE HAD BEEN HOME from prison for several months. He was on a number of medications prescribed by the doctors in Baltimore and they seemed to be helping. According to Sonny, his dad was getting stronger every day. Being with Mae and Sonny and looking forward to his first Thanksgiving at home in nine years, Al was a happy man. Al's mother had

Happy at home on Palm Island Al with his mother, Teresa

been down a couple of times over that first year at home and between her cooking and Mae's, he was putting on weight rapidly. In those days it was assumed that extra weight was an indication of prosperity and good health. By that measure, Al was healthier than he had ever been in his life.

He swam every day, had meals with his family and had time to read and reflect in a completely protected environment. Never again would he have to look over his shoulder wary of an assassin's bullet. Contrary to all that has been written about Al missing Chicago and the life he had led, he told his son he did not miss Chicago at all. His comment repeatedly to Sonny was, "they can give it back to the Indians for all I care".

More importantly to him, Al felt that he had made peace with God. Whether this was the answer to Mae and his mother's years of prayer for his soul or more the impact of the desperate catharsis that had occurred when he was in solitary, or both, Al felt he had been given another chance at life. He meant to enjoy every moment of it and no one was better at enjoying life than Al. To Mae's great joy, he was even attending mass with her at St. Patrick's regularly. Often they went several times each week. Al sat in the alcove near the Blessed Mother Mary's statue and did not go forward when Holy Communion was distributed at mass. Father Barry, who was the pastor of St. Patrick's Church, had been very kind to him and Al didn't want to take a chance on doing anything that might draw attention to his presence or cause embarrassment to the saintly priest. Father Barry had told both Mae and Al on numerous occasions that if anyone is truly sorry for their sins and willing to amend their life, no matter how grievous the sin might be, those sins will be forgiven. "That is the promise that Christ made to mankind when he was alive on earth two thousand years ago", Father Barry said. Al drew great consolation from this message of hope and was committed to living each of his days, however many that might be, making amends for his sins and with love and gratitude for his second chance.

It was enough for him now that he could be present with Mae in this beautiful Catholic Church that was the heart of the parish where Sonny had graduated high school. He didn't want to think about all those years that he had missed or all those special occasions and holidays that occurred while he was far away. He also did not want to think about where he had been. All that was in the past and he didn't plan to ever be away again.

After his first few months at home on Palm Island during which he had opened his heart to Mae and talked about his life and all that he had experienced in prison, he never wanted to think about any of the last nine years again. For that matter, he had closed the door on all of his public life and was determined to focus on the present and the glorious future he anticipated with his growing family. Casey and Jim were the newest members. They were at the house several times each week and Al understood his son's attraction to Casey. Al thought of her as the daughter he had never had. Sonny's devotion to Jim was also touching. Jim was the little brother he had never had and for Al, too, spending time with Jim helped assuage the grief he felt for those missed years with Sonny. Jim was exactly the age Sonny had been when Al first went away.

Al was particularly grateful that he was completely removed from involvement in his old life. Ralph had assured him that he had nothing to worry about. Ralph said he would send money regularly to Mae as he had while Al was away and there was plenty to cover whatever they needed. He said, "You have taken care of the family long enough, now is time for you to relax and let me take care of you." That seemed to suit Al just fine. All the drive and ambition of his youth were gone. When some of his friends came from Chicago to visit they were so shocked by his changed demeanor that they assumed he must have lost his mind. Little did they know or understand his transformation. Al was happy to let them think whatever they wanted and say whatever they wanted as long as it allowed him a reprieve from the dark world he had escaped. Many of his old friends who weren't imprisoned or dead still lived in that dark world.

As Thanksgiving approached so did the one-year anniversary of the date he had been released from prison. All those years of sadness and fear were behind him now. He smiled at Mae as she rambled on about all the family and friends who would be gathering for their big celebration. Casey and her little brother would be joining them. Mae loved Casey too, but Al knew that when Sonny announced the coming marriage, it would be hard for her. Mae had told him, this last year with Sonny and Al at home with her had been the best year of her life. Any change in that domestic bliss would not be welcomed by his beloved wife.

From the moment Al met Mae, he had thought she was the most beautiful girl he had ever seen. Now as they grew older, he saw a deeper beauty and strength of character in her that he didn't know she possessed. He would do anything to keep her happy and knew that when the time came to discuss Sonny's marriage, he would have to use every ounce of charisma he still possessed to help her let go of her precious son. Mae loved being the most important woman in their little world and making room for Casey would be a difficult challenge. He resolved to deal with that issue when the time came. Al thought back to their early years of their marriage and the days when he and Mae had called themselves "Maggie and Jiggs" after the popular funny paper characters and their precious Sonny they always called "Jiggy". It was just the three of them in their own little world. Yes, he knew there would be challenges ahead, but for now he wanted Mae to be happy even if it meant pretending for just a little while longer that "it was just the three of them". Al reveled in the pleasure of his loved ones' company and the holiday preparations.

Al and Mae Capone, Palm Island 1942

There would be a full house for Thanksgiving and more than at any time he could remember, Al had much to be thankful for and he knew it.

Casey's journal reflects the same sentiment that Al had expressed. _Thanksgiving 1940:_ _"What a day! I won't eat again for a week. We had a big turkey dinner at my mother's house and then went over later that afternoon to have another turkey dinner at Sonny's parents' house. We have much to be thankful for."_

Casey continued keeping a journal over the coming years, and recounted numerous gatherings at the Capone home. She said it was always a pleasure being around Uncle Al. Many years later when she heard people talk about how mentally impaired Al had become, she said that she found that quite puzzling. She said that she found the opposite to be true. She repeated the same story that her brother Jim had told me about how amazing it was to watch Uncle Al play cards. She said there were many times when guests filled several tables on the spacious porches, all playing gin rummy or pinochle or hearts. Al could keep track of which card everyone had played and what each players score was without writing anything down. This instant recall was always a source of amazement to all who observed it. Casey said she never witnessed any mental impairment or erratic behavior.

The following entry particularly reflects Casey's sensitivity to both Al and Mae's feelings about the upcoming wedding. It also paints a picture of a young woman who wanted very much to be accepted into the Capone family. Never one time in any of her journals did Casey express concern about marrying into the family of the notorious Al Capone. What is even more surprising is that no one in her family expressed reservations either. Family members have all indicated that from the first time Sonny Capone came into their lives, everyone loved him. After years of knowing and loving Sonny, it just did not seem to matter who his father was.

November 27, 1941: _"Thanksgiving Day and my 22nd_
birthday. "From the moment I awakened this morning,
I was filled with excitement and anticipation. We would
be having dinner at my mother's home and then go to
the Capone's. We had announced our engagement ear-
lier this fall. Uncle Al was delighted. Aunt Mae wept. I
knew she didn't dislike me. She just did not want Sonny
to marry and leave home. Sonny and I decided as
homage to his parents, we would plan our wedding for
December 30, which was their 23rd wedding anniversa-
ry. We were so happy. We wanted his mother to be happy
too. Now the wedding invitations have arrived and we
will present one to Sonny's parents at the dinner. All the
others have been addressed and will go into the mail on
Monday. I know Uncle Al is happy about the wedding. I
so hope Aunt Mae will be too."

> Mrs. Ruth Martin Casey
> requests the honour of your presence
> at the marriage of her daughter
> Diana Ruth Casey
> to
> Mr. Albert Francis Capone
> on Tuesday, the thirtieth of December
> at ten o'clock in the morning
> Saint Patrick's Church
> Miami Beach, Florida

December 7, 1941: "I am in a state of shock. Everyone is except the sneaky Japanese military. It is Sunday afternoon and I was shopping in Burdines Department Store in downtown Miami. It is a lovely store and, of course, filled with Christmas decorations at this joyous time of year. Christmas music was playing and I was finishing up shopping for my trousseau and last minute Christmas presents. I was feeling so happy. I remember exactly where I was standing on my way down the escalator, when the music stopped. A few seconds went by and then a man's loud voice announced that early this morning the Japanese had bombed the U. S. Naval Base at Pearl Harbor, Hawaii. He said several people including civilians were dead. Everyone gasped. Some began to cry and a few began speaking hysterically. It is the first time in my life that I felt absolute terror. I immediately left the store. All I could think was I had to get home and call Sonny."

December 29, 1941: "This is the last night I will spend in my mother's house. Tomorrow is our wedding day. Sonny and I are so excited and happy about being together at last. It is hard, though, to put out of our minds that our country is at war. Many of our friends and family have already enlisted. I know it is selfish, but I am so glad Sonny is seriously hearing impaired and won't have to go. My little brother is too young so, thank God, I won't have to worry about him either. Christmas was a very subdued affair for everyone and we look forward to our wedding, but also are feeling sadness and concern for our loved ones and the whole world. The world is at war and all I can do is pray. I also feel such sadness that my father

won't be here for my wedding. It is the most impor-
tant day of my life and he is not coming. His older
brother, my Uncle Dan Casey, will walk me down
the aisle. My parents divorced a few years ago, but I
never dreamed that my father wouldn't be here for
my wedding. Mother is putting on a bright face, but
I know she is very sad too. So much sadness on what
should be the happiest day of my life."

Casey & Sonny, Wedding Day,
12/30/1941

"Casey" - a beautiful bride in 1941

Sonny and Casey home from their honeymoon with Al and Mae 1942

chapter twenty

THE BEST TIMES
OF THEIR LIVES

MAE WATCHED AL AS HE sat quietly on the boat dock watching the boats go by and enjoying the gentle breezes from Biscayne Bay. He appeared to be a man who had found true peace. In fact he had. He told Mae he had never felt such a sense of well-being and he thanked God for these days of contentment. Mae thought back over the last few months and counted her blessings as well. Al's health issues had diminished. The doctors said there was no way of knowing how long this period would last, and ultimately the prognosis was not good, but for now his condition was relatively stable. He was sleeping better and loved the gentle pace of their days with the coming and going of loved ones.

All the family had gathered in Florida at the end of December to celebrate the wedding of Sonny to Casey. They were perfect together and Al was thankful that Mae had seen that and been able to welcome Casey to the family. The wedding was held at St. Patrick's Church in Miami Beach. Casey was the most beautiful bride Al had ever seen and everyone could see that the young couple was deeply in love. Casey's mother, Ruth, had spent a fortune on the elaborate reception which was held at a private club in Miami Beach to afford the family, all their guests and especially Al, the utmost seclusion from the public.

Despite the horror of the war, which was, of course, all anyone could talk about at that time, at this moment, Al said he felt removed from the turmoil of the rest of the world and very happy to have survived his own war. He rarely thought back to those awful years during Prohibition or to the days when he was in prison and removed from all he loved. When he did think of the past, it was as if it had all happened to another person. The fear, the brutality, the nightmare of it all had been lifted from him. He knew how lucky he was to have found this peace and he frequently talked about it with Mae.

Just then, the phone rang and Mae called to him, "Al come to the phone, Sonny is calling from Colorado," Al hastened to the house filled with anticipation to take a call from Sonny and Casey, who were taking an extended trip across the West ultimately to pay a visit to Henry Clark, who was in the Navy. Henry, Muriel and Louie's son, would be shipping out from San Diego to join the war effort in the South Pacific. As Al took the phone a look of pure joy covered his face. Since it was summer time and school was out, Sonny had insisted that they take Casey's brother, Jim, with them. Jim was obsessed with cowboys and the Wild West and Sonny wanted to share their adventure with him. Al too was very fond of Jim and he was anxious to hear how the little guy was enjoying the trip. After a few minutes of delightful details, he said, "I love you, son of my heart" and passed the phone back to an impatient Mae. Later, when it was just the two of them, they talked into the night about how blessed they had been to have such a wonderful son and now a daughter as well. They even speculated about how many grandchildren they would have, something they both anticipated. "A half a dozen would be great," Al told her. "Oh Fonzie, you are too much," she said. "Well Josie, we can hope can't we." These special nicknames they had for each other were only known to the immediate family and saved for the happiest of occasions.

As summer wore on, Sonny and Casey had returned to Florida after their four-week trip to the west filled with colorful details about their adventure. They were especially glad they had had an opportunity to see Henry in San Diego before he shipped out. In the meantime, Muriel and Louis had rented out their home in Chicago and had become permanent residents with Al and Mae on Palm Island. Everyone was happy about that.

Months went by and it was now well into 1942. Sonny and Casey had just purchased a little white bungalow in nearby Miami Shores, which Al always referred to as "the little white house". Sonny had begun working at the military ammunition facility in South Miami. His hearing disability resulted in his classification as 4F, but he was happy that at least he could support the war effort at the military depot.

Then at last, Sonny and Casey gave them the news they had been greatly anticipating, Al and Mae would become grandparents in early 1943. They both were ecstatic and immediately began the conversation about gender and possible names for the newest family member. Even with the war raging, these were happy years for Al and Mae. Family and friends came and went, and Al said over and over, "how good life was."

Once in a while, despite Al's disdain for Chicago and his bad memories, he and Mae drove up to the city with Muriel and Louis. Since many members of their families were still living in Chicago, he did agree to short and surreptitious visits.

Ralph had purchased property in rural Wisconsin close to a town called Mercer, which was not a long drive from Chicago. Whenever he learned that his brother would be coming to Chicago, Ralph invited Al up to visit. Al loved being in his brother's lodge in this beautiful part of the country especially when Ralph tempted him with long days of fishing, which Al enjoyed. Mae acquiesced to these fishing expeditions on two occasions, but usually discouraged them for a couple of reasons. Over the years since Al's return to Florida, Ralph and Mae's relationship had grown more and more acrimonious. Ralph wanted to be in charge of Al's life and considered himself the boss of the family. Mae told me that Ralph had always been

Al Capone, Wisconsin 1946

a bully and a chauvinist, and while Al was away she tolerated him for the sake of peace in the family. Now that Al was home, she was determined to be in charge of his care and she was not going to let anyone disrupt their peaceful household.

Ralph was never a warm man and as he had gotten older he seemed to have become increasingly bitter. He would never be the man his brother was; he was not as brilliant, not as powerful, and certainly not as big hearted and loved. Al's doctors had told Mae they would not deal with Ralph at all. They found him to be a pompous and argumentative know-it-all, and they preferred consulting directly with her without Ralph's involvement. Mae agreed, and relied on Al's younger brothers John and Mattie as much as possible when she needed help with Al's care. The other reason why she was never comfortable and always apprehensive when Ralph was around was that he tended to incite agitation in Al. He liked to talk about the old days in Chicago and often suggested that Al return to the old life. On at least one occasion, Al became so provoked that he and Ralph had a physical altercation and the other brothers had to intervene to quell the conflict. When Mae heard about this she made sure that Al did not go up to Wisconsin again unless she was present.

On one of Al's two fishing trips to Wisconsin, his long-lost brother reappeared. It was Vincenzo, the eldest of the family, whom Al had not seen since his disappearance over 30 years before. He had been sixteen when he ran away from New York. There are various stories about why, but whatever the reason, he stayed away for years. Vincenzo Capone, called Jimmy by his brothers, had changed his name to Richard Hart and lived in the Western states and most recently in Nebraska. He worked for much of his life in law enforcement. He also spent many years as an Indian agent, and was well respected by the Indians as a white man who kept his word. To some Indians, he was considered a brother. Throughout his life, Vincenzo had never told his real name to anyone, not even his wife and four sons. During the Depression in the thirties, Richard Hart, as he was now known, fell on very hard times. Despite a lifetime away from the Capone family, he had turned in desperation to them for help. He was welcomed back with open arms. In the Capone family, no explanation was necessary. He was home, he was welcomed and he was given the financial assistance he needed.

Al, who had been in prison at the time when his older brother returned to the family, was overjoyed. Eventually at Al's invitation, Jimmy came for an extended visit to the house on Palm Island where at last the brothers could have a chance to become fully reacquainted. For Al, loyalty to family was absolute. Though he didn't convey much from his private conversations with his older brother to Mae, she later recalled the visits as warm and very cordial. She said she liked Jimmy and knew Al was delighted to have his brother back. Even after their reunion, however, Jimmy was reluctant to fully disclose his real identity when he returned home. After a lifetime of living as Richard Hart and lying to his immediate family and everyone he knew, it was difficult for him to admit now that he was the older brother of Al Capone, a man once known as public enemy Number One.

These years of peace and tranquility on Palm Island were filled with many happy gatherings, stories of which were passed down through the years. One of our particular favorites was the one that our Uncle Jim loved to tell of the time Mama Mae had gone to run errands with her sister, Muriel and her husband, Louie. Al had been left alone in the house. Brown was there, but he was working in the garden. This incident occurred in the early 1940's while World War II was going on and there were a number of military bases in Florida. On this afternoon while Papa was alone, two Army Air Force pilots from a nearby air base, on a dare from their buddies, climbed over the wall and onto the grounds of the Capone home. The young soldiers entered the property and were surprised to find there were no armed guards. There were no big dogs for protection. There was nothing but lush gardens and gentle breezes. Their buddies would never believe they had gotten onto the estate of Al Capone without being apprehended or even noticed, or so they thought. As they skirted the edge of the big house heading toward the pool area, a friendly voice called out, "Hi boys, would you like a cold beer?" They stopped in their tracks and slowly turned toward the voice of the heavy set man who was lounging on the screen porch. They knew instantly it was Al Capone. "Oh, sorry to disturb you Mr. Capone, I guess we are a little lost", they said. "You're not disturbing me, actually I would enjoy some company. Come on in and I'll pour you a cold one" their gracious host said. "The guys at the base are never going to believe this, one whispered to the other."

When Mama Mae returned home an hour later, she heard the men's voices coming from the largest of the porches. Her first instinct was fear. Had something happened to Al in her absence? What she found were two laughing young men in uniform with several empty beer bottles in front of them deeply engrossed in conversation with her husband, who appeared to be having the time of his life. "What's going on?" she asked coolly. The soldiers jumped to their feet, as Al smiled up at her and said, "Mae, I'm just entertaining some troops who lost their way". Mae did not think the situation very amusing and she didn't hesitate to make her feelings clear. She said, "I don't think your commanding officer will find this very amusing either when I call him." "Now Mae, that won't be necessary. There's no harm done and I'm sure it will never happen again," Al said. "No ma'am, Mrs. Capone, sorry to disturb you," they apologized. "Thanks for the beer, Mr. Capone. It was nice talking with you," they said as they headed for the door. Al said, "By the way boys, you can use the gate, no need to climb back over the wall." he grinned. "Thank you, sir" could be heard as they quickly left the premises. Uncle Jim said Papa loved to tell that story and always laughed when he did, eventually Mama Mae laughed too.

Unfortunately, the days of peace and joy went all too fast. Al had come home to Palm Island in the winter of 1940.

He often told everyone repeatedly that those wonderful years with Mae, Sonny, the extended family and friends, and especially his precious granddaughters were the happiest of his life. Yes, he had times when his health was a problem, but he had good doctors and received good care. It had been years since he had any contact with his former business associates. Once it became clear that he was no longer the "Al Capone" of his earlier days of gangland triumph, they stayed away. At night, he was rarely troubled with the nightmares of his youth.

One benefit of his chronic illness was his diminished recall of the worst parts of his life, especially the constant fear of being killed. He lived totally in the present. He had made his peace with God. Each day he arose from his bed knowing that Mae was there and she filled his days with laughter and affection. After he kissed Mae "good morning", his first question of the day was always, "are we going to the little white house or are the baby girls coming over here?"

It was 1947 and Al was celebrating his forty eighth birthday on the seventeenth of January. His little blue-eyed blond granddaughter, Diane, whom the family called "Pat", had turned three on the fourteenth and they were celebrating their birthdays together at a family dinner. He told everyone that his three granddaughters were the best birthday presents he had ever received. Mae brought in the beautiful big birthday cake with candles as everyone sang "Happy Birthday" to Papa and Pat.

Diane "Pat" Capone, Age 3

As Al lifted Pat into his lap so they could blow out the candles together, he thought again how lucky he was to be surrounded by so much peace and happiness. It was to be the last birthday party ever celebrated in the Capone dining room.

AFTERWARD

IN THE YEARS FOLLOWING PAPA'S death, our lives and that of Mama Mae's went on, but nothing was as it had been. His death had been devastating to all the family, but it was catastrophic for her. She had been attending to Papa's every need and desire and considered his care her primary purpose in life. For a long time after his death, it appeared that life had gone out of her as well. My father often said that if it had not been for her faith and the pleasure of being with her granddaughters, he was not sure that she would have wanted to go on.

Thankfully for all of us, she did get through those first terrible months and in time regained her cheerful disposition. She lived for almost forty years after Papa's death and never stopped missing him or speaking devotedly of him. She also never took off her wedding rings.

Mama Mae was a wonderful grandmother. We felt so fortunate to have her and her wonderful stories, which kept Papa alive for all of us as we grew up.

AUTHOR'S NOTES

INTRODUCTION

1. In the years after Al Capone's death in 1947 both Mae and Sonny Capone were offered large amounts of money on numerous occasions to tell their stories and they repeatedly refused. Both could have used additional resources, but both chose to live modestly and keep family stories private.

CHAPTER 1

1. Dr. Kenneth Phillips was the primary Capone family physician in Miami, Florida from 1928 when the family moved to the Palm Island home until after the death of Al Capone in January 1947. Afterwards, he continued to care for Mae and Sonny Capone's family intermittently for a number of years. Dr. Phillips signed Al Capone's death certificate which stated that the primary cause of death was "bronchial pneumonia 48 hours contributing apoplexy 4 days". He had suffered what was then called an apoplectic stroke on Tuesday, January 21, 1947. After fourteen hours in a coma, he rallied, regained consciousness and began to improve. Then on Friday he developed pneumonia. Finally on Saturday, January 25, at 7:25 p. m. he succumbed to cardiac arrest. Al Capone, who for many years feared being shot down and killed on the street, died at home in his own bed after receiving the blessings of the Catholic Church and surrounded by his loved ones.

CHAPTER 4

1. Al Capone and Mary Josephine (Mae) Coughlin Capone grew up 1.3 miles apart in Brooklyn, N. Y. He lived at 38

Garfield Place in a predominantly Italian neighborhood and she at 117 3rd Place in an Irish neighborhood. Despite the proximity of their homes, they lived in very different worlds and did not meet until early 1918.

2. Vincenzo Capone (Al's oldest brother, who was called Jimmy by his brothers) was known as Richard "Two Gun" James Hart by the rest of the world. The stories of Vincenzo were shared with me by my cousin Richard Corey Hart. In 2013, a book entitled Two Gun Hart was written and published by Jeff McArthur with the assistance of my cousins: Corey, his father, Jeff and his grandfather, Harry Hart. It is a carefully documented and well written story of Vincenzo's life. Harry is Vincenzo's youngest son and he was kind enough to chat with me when I first began working on my book. Getting to meet and know my Hart cousins has been one of the nicest gifts I've received while writing the story of my family.

3. Most of the stories of Al Capone as a child were told to me by my father, Sonny. Many of them were told to me repeatedly when I was growing up. Sonny said that the story in Chapter 4 about Al's mother telling him when he was eleven years old that his father's health was not good and that she needed his help was told to him by Al personally. Sonny said many of these other stories about Al's childhood had also been told to him directly by his father. My grandmother, Mae, told me that Al's mother Teresa told her that Al always gave the money he made as a child to her.

CHAPTER 6

1. Al personally told Sonny the story of Mae's mother, Bridget Coughlin, hitting him with the broom and chasing him off the Coughlin's family porch when Al went to ask permission to marry Mae in 1918.

2. The story of my great grandmother, Bridget Coughlin saving my father's life when he was born prematurely on December 4, 1918, has been part of our family lore from earliest memory. Sonny, who became a large man as an adult frequently joked about the fact that "I started out in life weighing barely two pounds". Bridget who attended his birth at the Coughlin home wrapped the newborn in a wool blanket and placed him in a box on the opened door of the oven. My grandmother, Mae, said later when the doctor arrived at the family home he credited Bridget with saving Sonny's life.

CHAPTER 8

1. Ralphie Capone was the son of Ralph Capone and therefore Al's nephew. He grew up in the house that Al and Mae bought on Prairie Avenue in Chicago with the Capone family after he had been abandoned by his mother. Ralphie dropped the Capone name and used his middle name "Gabriel" as his surname after he finished college and throughout his adult life. I had the pleasure of meeting his grandson, Brian Gabriel during the writing of this book. Brian was kind enough in many wonderful phone conversations to tell me about his family, particularly his beloved paternal grandmother, Betty. Betty also went by the name Gabriel as did both of their children: Deirdre and Dennis. Dennis, who is now deceased, was Brian's father.

CHAPTER 11

1. The photograph of Charles "Lucky" Luciano that appears in this chapter was taken during a visit he made to Palm Island in 1929. Photo was taken by Al Capone.

CHAPTER 12

1. The story Sonny told me about being at a baseball game with his father when President Hoover appeared might have been misremembered. My father said he recalled people cheering his father and booing the president. Sonny thought this

might have precipitated the President's direction to the IRS and FBI to "get Capone". In researching this recounted event at a baseball game and discussing it with John Binder, the pre-eminent Capone historian, it appears that my father's recollection might be confused with another time when Hoover and Al were at a train station at the same time and some cheering occurred. There is no record of Al and the President ever being present at the same baseball game. Sonny was a young boy who loved his father and was emotionally distraught over the events leading up to his father's incarceration. Even though he told me this story with great specificity, it appears likely now that the two events were somewhat confused and misremembered.

CHAPTER 13

1. Al Capone was tried and convicted of income tax evasion in 1931. Before the trial many of his friends and family who feared what was to come, urged him to flee the country. He could have done so and lived lavishly as an expatriate in a number of other countries. Al vehemently rejected this proposal. His refusal was based on a number of factors: first, Al was basically an optimist and never anticipated the harsh sentence he was to be given. Secondly, America was his home. He was proud of being an American and he would never agree to leave his home. Third and finally, Al saw himself as a "stand-up" guy. To run away would be unmanly and cowardly. He had many flaws but being a coward wasn't one of them.

2. Al Capone was sent to the Federal Penitentiary in Atlanta in May 1932. It was here that he was officially diagnosed with syphilis after being given a Wasserman test (this test was previously used to identify syphilis and was routinely given to all incoming prisoners). It was never conclusively determined when the infection occurred, but was thought to have taken place when he was much younger (possibly in his late teen

years) as a result of one of his many sexual dalliances. It is likely he was not aware that he carried the dread disease and had been carrying it for many years. Syphilis progresses from the initial infection which is manifested by an open sore on the genitalia to a latent stage and ultimately after many years to the tertiary stage which kills an unlucky twenty percent of those infected.

CHAPTER 18

1. Casey, Al's daughter-in-law, is quoted in her journals expressing sadness that her father James F. Casey would not be in Miami Beach to walk her down the aisle at her wedding. Casey's parents had gone through a divorce a few years prior to Casey and Sonny's wedding and her father had quickly married his second wife. For a number of years after his remarriage he was estranged from both Casey and her brother. It was not until twenty years later that a complete family reconciliation occurred. James, his second wife, Jerry, and Casey's mother, Ruth, became close friends in the last days of James Casey's life.

*Throughout the 1980's many changes occurred in the family. In 1986, my grandmother, Mae Capone, passed away. At that point, she was the only member of the family who still used the Capone surname. The Capone name, however, was far from forgotten. The NBC network scheduled a two hour live broadcast for the evening of April 21, 1986 during which workers with jack hammers would dig their way into Al Capone's sealed vault under the Lexington Hotel in Chicago. The Lexington Hotel had been a headquarters of my grandfather and "the Outfit" fifty years before. For weeks leading up to the television special, Geraldo Rivera and the network went overboard hyping the opening of the secret vault. They speculated that the vault was filled with Al Capone's fortune which had been stashed there prior to his death in 1947. They also hinted that there might be bodies of Al's enemies along with machine guns and other gangland memorabilia. Geraldo managed to talk his way through two hours of prime time while the audiences, both in the U. S. and in twenty other countries around the world where it was being broadcast, sat riveted to their televisions. That evening my dad, Sonny, sat calmly in my home in California watching the spectacle. Finally, I asked him, "Do you think they will find anything, Daddy?" My dad said, "Oh yeah sure they will." I was shocked and asked, "Really?" He said, "Yeah, when they finally break through and flash the spotlight, there will be a big sign that says, "Fuck you, Geraldo!" signed Al Capone."

Acknowledgements

I HAVE BEEN TRYING TO write this book for several years and would never have finished it without the help and support of my family and friends. I started and stopped a number of times in tears of frustration. Over and over again whenever I felt ready to give up someone would reach out with a word of encouragement and I would be on my way again. I have received extraordinary kindness from so many people, some of whom I didn't even know until I began to write.

My project began over six years ago. I have seen and heard so many inaccurate tales about my family, particularly about my grandfather over the course of my life. I finally decided that I was the only member of his family alive who knew the truth, so it was up to me to tell it. From the first day I began, my husband, Don, whom I call my dear Editor-in-Chief, was by my side encouraging me. He has read and reread this book so many times I think he knows it by heart.

Right after I began, I had the great good fortune of meeting two gifted writers who were also doing research on my grandfather in preparation for books of their own. They are John J. Binder who subsequently wrote the quintessential history of the Prohibition era called, Al Capone's Beer Wars and Deirdre Bair, who first interviewed me in 2012 in preparation for her book, Al Capone: His Life, Legacy, and Legend, which is the most comprehensive biography ever written about my grandfather. Both are scholars who had done exhaustive research on the man I called "Papa" and both of them supported me and my project from the very first conversations we had. Both have generously helped me through this sometimes overwhelming process and have become trusted friends.

Deirdre Bair didn't just mentor me, she recruited many of her closest friends to assist me as well. From the very gracious Sydney Stern to the brilliant Mary Lawrence Test, who dropped her own projects to Copy Edit my manuscript, and others in between, I have been awed by the number of highly accomplished women friends of Deirdre's who have helped me along the way.

One of the most rewarding outcomes of my project has been getting to know some of my Capone cousins: Dr. Richard Corey Hart, his father Jeff and his grandfather, Harry, and also Brian Gabriel. Reconnecting with my dear cousin Mike Martin, who was such a big part of my childhood, and renewing our bond was a particular joy. We will always be grateful to Mario Gomes of the Al Capone Museum for his many kindnesses to our family over the years.

Big thanks go to Nicholas D. Wells, my intellectual property rights attorney, who keeps me and my writing safe. Thank you to Jessika Hazelton, Meradith and all the gifted professionals at The Troy Book Makers for their artistry and diligence in turning my manuscript into a book I am proud of. Special thanks to Suzanne Gove-O'Rourke, Dr. Patrice Des Pois, and Dr. Mark Knoble for keeping me fit and healthy over the years it took me to complete this labor of love.

There have been so many of my loved ones: Gordon Peterson, America Francis, George Prince, Theresa Hall, Katherine Bayley, Carol and Hal Toppel, Joni Johnson and Tom Coons, Nancy and Ron Kelly, Mary Graves, Susan Holding, Bill Beck, Jo Beck, Al and Laura Enamait, Barbara and Bob Felder, Tom Smith, my soul sisters: Margie Smith, Mary Cloud, Kimberly Sanders, Paula Tischler Watson, Dr. Jean Neil, my Chicago cousins, Clairmae and Don, my Uncle Jim Casey along with all the Casey family in Florida and all five of our children and their families including my beloved grandchildren who have taken turns holding my hands and offering words of encouragement throughout this writing journey.

The greatest love and gratitude goes to my dear sister, Barbara Prince, without whom this book would never have made it from my computer to the publisher. She saved me and all my work more times than I can count. She and Don are the two people most responsible for the completion of this book and to whom I owe my deepest thanks.

BIBLIOGRAPHY

Bair, Deirdre, <u>CAPONE His Life, Legacy and Legend</u>, copyright 2016

Bergreen, Laurence, <u>CAPONE, The Man and the Era</u>, copyright 1994

Binder, John J. , <u>AL CAPONE'S BEER WARS</u>, copyright 2017

Kobler, John, <u>CAPONE, The Life and World of Al Capone</u>, copyright 1971

Pasley, Fred D. , <u>AL CAPONE: The Biography of a Self-Made Man,</u> copyright 1930

Schoenberg, Robert J. , <u>MR. CAPONE</u>, copyright 1992

GROWING UP CAPONE

IN THE COMING MONTHS, A second book written by Diane Patricia Capone called **Growing Up Capone** will be released. This second book discusses the impact of his legacy on his descendants and what happened to the family in the years after Al Capone died.

Made in the USA
Monee, IL
26 December 2021

87126454R40095